THE EVERYDAY WHOLEFOOD COOKBOOK

Healthy Meals for All the Family

Edited by Ruth Lea

Published in association with
La Leche League (Great Britain)

GRUB STREET · LONDON

Published by Grub Street
The Basement, 10 Chivalry Road
London SW11 1HT

British Library Cataloguing in Publication Data
The everyday wholefood cookbook: healthy meals for all the family
   1. Cookery (Natural foods)
   I. Lea, Ruth II. La Leche League (Great Britain)
   641.5'637

ISBN 1 898697 55 8

Edited by Ruth Lea
Illustrations by Madeleine David
Cover photograph by Tim Imrie
Other photographs by John Morrice
Food preparation and styling by Carol Bowen
Designed and formatted by Adam Denchfield
Printed and bound in Great Britain by Biddles Ltd, Guildford and King's Lynn

Contents

ACKNOWLEDGEMENTS

The recipes in this book are those of the mothers of La Leche League of Great Britain. I would like to thank everyone who sent me their favourite recipes and offered suggestions and help and in particular:

Dr David L. J. Freed, MB, MD, MI Biol Allergist and Professional Advisor to LLLGB for writing the section on Breast Feeding and Food Allergy. Mary May, for her contribution to the section on Guidelines for a Balanced Healthy Diet.

CONTRIBUTORS

Caroline Ambrose, Sue Asquith, Helena Boutal, M. Brown, Sue Cardus, Esther Culpin, Sue Darkins, Avril Dawson, Liz Denno, Ginny Eaton, Helen Ellery, Linda Evans, Susie Everington, Allison Fallowfield, Anne Gaskell, Dorothy Goodey, Judy Greef, Deirdre Hayton, Lorraine Hogg, Dorothy Howell, Judith Hughes, Sue Hunter, Sandra Irving, Diana James, Ros Kane, Penny Kurowski, Linda Lawrence, Margaret Mairura, Tessa Merrett, Tracy Newman-Ford, Alison Onyelekere, Sarah Palmer, Jane Pearson, Romsey LLL, Rachel Scrafield, Anne Sladen, Caryl Stock, Cynthia Turner, Lyn Walcott, Myra Yeo.

TESTERS

Sue Asquith, Julie Bateman, Sarah Brown, Liz Denno, Helen Ellery, Mike Ellery, Lesley Harrison, Ros Kane, Linda Lawrence, Tessa Merret, Anne Thurlow, Cynthia Turner.

OTHER HELP

Mary Cryan, Jill Dye, Leslie Fickling, Daphne Ford, Sheila Wells, and last but certainly not least, Terry, Rachel, Ian and Alan.

Calcium exchanges reproduced by kind permission of The National Dairy Council.

Anne Dolamore and the Grub Street team for supporting the project with suggestions and advice.

Preface

This recipe book celebrates twenty-five years of La Leche League in Great Britain, from the time our first leader started to help mothers breastfeed their babies. Since then we have grown to become a national registered charity dedicated to offering mother-to-mother support to women who have chosen to breastfeed.

These mothers know they are giving their babies THE superior infant food. Breast milk supplies the perfect balance of nutrients to promote the baby's health, development and growth. Mothers want to ensure that their babies and older children continue to receive as nutritious a diet as possible, from the moment they start to show interest in trying foods other than breast milk, usually in the second half of their first year.

Mothers often ask us what they can feed their families, that doesn't break the bank, tastes good, does them good and is easy to prepare when there is a baby, toddler and perhaps also older children to care for.

LA LECHE LEAGUE PHILOSOPHY

The League philosophy on nutrition offers an answer. It provides a simple and straightforward yardstick by which we can all assess our diets. It can be broken down into two simple rules:

1. A well-balanced and varied diet basically means eating as many different things as possible, never too much of the same thing.
2. Eat things in as close to their natural state as possible. This means avoiding highly processed foods where possible, and reducing preparation and cooking which destroys some nutrients. Of course foods which may carry infection, such as meat and fish, have to be well enough cooked to destroy the organisms, but most vegetables can be eaten virtually raw.

But how can we put this into practice? Small steps at a time are the best way. Huge overnight dietary changes tend not to last!

For example, it doesn't take much effort while shopping to look in the trolley and think 'Am I buying a wide range of foods here? Can I increase the variety of my diet by buying something new today?' Also try looking at the food on your plate and think: 'Could I buy or cook this next time in such a way as to leave it closer to its natural state?' Sometimes the answer will be 'No', sometimes 'Yes, but I can't afford to; or I don't have time, or I can't be bothered', (total honesty here) but from time to time you should be able to say 'Yes' and you can take a step towards improving your diet.

BASIC RULES TO IMPROVE YOUR FAMILY'S DIET

The beauty of this is that no matter how good or poor your diet is to start with, you can use these basic rules to make improvements. If natural wholefoods have not been part of your normal family diet, introduce them gradually. Simply having plenty of fresh salads or vegetables with a meal, and fruit afterwards, is a good start. Carefully reducing the amount of sugar you use, and replacing it with unrefined golden granulated sugar or honey can be quite painless. The gradual introduction of wholemeal flour by using it half-and-half with white flour in baking is often acceptable. Beans and lentils can be added to soups and casseroles in small quantities.

One way is to think of the chain of changes an item of food goes through from its 'natural state' to arriving on your plate and see if you can move back along the chain a bit. For example, instead of serving frozen fish fingers, you might ask a fishmonger for freshly-made fish cakes. This would give you the opportunity, if you wanted, to ask about what was in them. Another step back along this chain would be to buy the fish and make your own fish cakes. Next would be to buy the fish and 'process' it less by cooking it as it is. If you want to go further you could maybe go fishing and catch the fish yourself! No, we're not being silly, the point we're trying to make is that this principle can apply to everyone and each of us can decide how far we can go at any one time.

Another example is yoghurt. Many people buy this, thinking it is 'healthy', but if they realised how much sugar is in most pots of flavoured yoghurt they might choose to buy a chocolate pudding instead! How about buying unflavoured, unsweetened natural yoghurt and adding your own flavourings? Puréed or chopped fruit and honey are good. Even if you have to add some sugar, at least you will know how much and could choose unrefined cane sugar Instead of white. Or the next step would be to make your own yoghurt... yoghurt makers are not expensive and very easy to use.

How about breakfast cereal closer to its natural state? You could use rolled oats to make a quick porridge or go a bit further with pinhead oatmeal which needs to be soaked overnight, then boiled a while. Again, even if you have to serve it with sugar, at least you are in control of how much. Small changes, such as buying some fresh fruit instead of tinned; or even fruit tinned in fruit juice rather than syrup, will make a significant improvement to some people's diets, whereas others may be taking the step of buying organic vegetables, or growing their own. Everyone can use these simple rules to make some improvements.

Of course this leaves plenty of room for personal taste and concerns. You can choose to avoid meat, but still should aim to eat a wide variety of other foods. Many people worry about the amount of sugar their children consume and so buy 'no added sugar' juices, whereas other people are more worried about the alternative sweeteners in those juices and prefer to have the sugar. A step in the right direction from either stance would be to buy natural juices with no additives, whenever you can afford to. On the subject of juice, I read a long time ago the theory that we shouldn't drink juice at all but instead eat the fruit itself. This gives us the same juice as well as nutrients and fibre in the fruit. I never thought much about this until last summer when, being pregnant, I found myself terribly thirsty in the warm weather. However, if I drank a big quantity of anything, I felt very sick. I tried frequent small drinks, juice, milk, water, tea, but nothing helped until I remembered this idea of eating the fruit instead of drinking the juice. I found an orange or juicy peach went a long way towards quenching my thirst, and if it was not enough I could follow it with a glass of water without the accustomed nausea. Of course it would be unrealistic in our society to expect everyone to eat fruit all the time instead of having a drink but it is an idea worth bearing in mind. Perhaps a young child who is reluctant to drink anything but sweetened juice might accept some chunks of orange rather than a drink of fresh orange juice.

How about food preparation and cooking? Try to steam vegetables instead of boiling them, and often we eat them raw. My eldest son, who has been a lifelong non-vegetable eater has responded to this in a big way and now loves carrots, broccoli and green beans...as long as they are not cooked! I've also started making some old-fashioned puddings for a treat instead of buying cakes. Things like rice pudding and semolina are not difficult to make and, by cutting down on the sugar and using semi-skimmed milk instead of full-cream, you can reduce their calorie and fat content.

The selection of recipes in this book has come from the mothers of La Leche League of Great Britain, and has been tasted and tested by them and their families. Some have been handed down through several generations, others have been developed from the cooking styles of the seventies, eighties and nineties.

Most of the recipes call for fresh ingredients and unrefined wholefoods, entirely in line with current advice about eating plenty of fruit and vegetables and unrefined carbohydrates. We find that many people embrace the wholefood concept enthusiastically, whereas others are less sure and need convincing. So you will find here recipes for all points on the wholefood continuum.

The message of this book is that to eat fresh food in as natural a state as possible, you need to start with the fresh unrefined ingredients, and make things yourself; AND THAT THIS IS POSSIBLE even when you have a young family to look after.

Ruth Lea and Lorna McMillan

The First Wholefood - Mother's Milk

Breastmilk is an amazing substance. It is the ideal food for a baby. What is more, a mother's milk is the most perfect milk for her own baby. It contains all the nutrients, proteins, minerals and vitamins, in just the right balance for the optimum growth and development of the baby. The milk of the mother of a premature baby is different from that of a full-term mother, to meet her baby's special growing needs. What is more, breastmilk is an active substance. The mother produces antibodies to infections to which she is exposed. This provides protection to the baby through her milk. Breastfed babies have fewer colds, tummy bugs, ear infections, or respiratory problems. They suffer less from allergic symptoms such as colic, runny nose, eczema, wheezing (or, if there is a tendency for such things in the family, being breastfed may at least delay the onset of such symptoms).

Breastmilk is the ultimate convenience food. There is no risk of contamination. It is always available to the baby from the mother at the right temperature, in the right amount, and in the right balance of fluid and nutrients. With no bottles to prepare, or feeding equipment to carry, travelling is easy. With practice, a mother needs only one arm to support the baby whilst breastfeeding. She can use the other hand to cuddle an older child (or write a letter, or make a phone call...)

The economy of breastfeeding is very attractive! No bottles, sterilizing equipment or milk powder to buy. No waste, as the baby gets just the right amount every time. No risk of making up feeds which are too strong or weak, or not needed. With planning and budgeting it costs very little extra to ensure the mother has a diet adequate to maintain her own good health whilst breastfeeding.

The emotional benefits of breastfeeding are boundless. As the mother and baby enjoy their close intimate contact they get the chance to know and love each other. As the baby feeds facing the mother, eye-to-eye contact is encouraged. The hormones of breastfeeding make the mother feel relaxed and motherly, particularly once lactation is established and settled. A breastfed baby even smells nice! The stools and any broughtback milk are inoffensive. Putting the baby to the breast for comfort, as well as for nourishment, provides the mother with an easy and effective way to soothe the baby anywhere, and this remains particularly helpful as the baby grows older.

In Great Britain the Department of Health recognizes the benefits of breastfeeding and recommends that babies continue to receive breastmilk throughout the first year. The World Health Organisation goes further, and recommends that babies receive breastmilk for at least two years.

How to Breastfeed

La Leche League devotes all its energies to helping mothers breastfeed their babies, and has an entire book on the subject, as well as many leaflets. So this is just a very brief outline about how to get started. For details of our publications, and your nearest La Leche League leader who can help you in your own special circumstances, contact the address at the back of this book.

- Enlist the unconditional support of your partner, family and health professionals.
- Be confident. For 99% of women there is no physical reason why they cannot breastfeed (it's what everyone did until very recently in our history).
- Be informed. Read our literature, or even better, attend our meetings to hear about and see breastfeeding firsthand.
- Relax.

The First Feeds

Most women have found that the two most important things about breastfeeding in the beginning are:

Breastfeed soon and breastfeed often

Studies have shown that the sooner you try to feed your baby after birth, the better; the baby's urge to suck is at its strongest in the first two hours or so after birth. The urge tends to diminish after that and may take about forty-eight hours to return. (But don't worry about it, just keep offering the breast to the baby).

Skin-to-skin contact helps to stimulate the milk supply, so for early feeds have as little clothing as possible between you and your baby. Hold the baby facing you so she doesn't have to turn her head, lining up her nose with your nipple. When the baby's mouth gapes wide open bring her to the breast quickly so that her chin touches the breast first. Her tongue will scoop up as much breast as possible and your nipple will be drawn well to the back of the mouth.

The baby will then start to "milk" the breast using a ripple action with the tongue and jaw. This will stimulate your hormones and the milk will start to flow.

Tiny babies have tiny tummies, and they can't wait long for food. Breast milk is digested easily and quickly, so your baby really is hungry often. Expect your baby to need to feed every two hours or so. Also, the baby's mouth is very important as a source of pleasure, and a way of finding out about things, so she may need to suck for reasons other than food. If you let your baby feed often you will find that

- you have plenty of milk - breastfeeding works as a demand and supply system, so that the more she feeds, the more milk there will be.
- you are less likely to have sore nipples - little and often is a good way to get your nipples used to being suckled. Sore nipples can often be relieved by adjusting the baby's latch-on position.
- engorgement can be lessened. A few days after your baby is born your breasts are likely to be very full and tender, as a result of your hormones working to produce your milk. Letting the baby suck often really will help to relieve your breasts and make them feel better.

New babies don't really know the difference between day and night, and it is logical that if they need to feed often in the day, they will need to feed often at night, too. This is not a problem for the breastfeeding mother who has the baby near to her in her room. Some find they can feed their babies when they need to at night, and hardly wake themselves.

Look after yourself. It is easy, in the excitement of the new baby's arrival, and anxiety to "get back to normal", to forget that you are tired or hungry and thirsty; this can make you feel low, and the baby quickly knows it. Remember to eat and drink. There are no foods you should not eat, though you may find your baby shows sensitivity to some, by being extra restless, or colicky. A good diet for the breastfeeding mother is the same as a good diet for anyone else, and the recipes in this book should give you some ideas using, for example, fresh fruit and vegetables, fish, meat, cheese, nuts, pulses, grains, wholemeal bread, pasta.

Some mothers make sure that in the morning they prepare a supply of cheese, or nuts, wholemeal bread, apples, bananas, dried fruit, ready to snack on during the day. They also have jugs or flasks of water or diluted fruit juice around the house. It is important to drink to your thirst.

Rest is a necessity, not a luxury. If your baby likes to suck a lot at a particular time of day (often afternoon or early evening) then let her. You can lie down with her in a dark quiet room, or sit with your feet up and watch TV or read a book. Thinking ahead, so that you have food in the freezer, or can prepare a meal early in the day, helps. A baby sling is a boon if you need to get things done. Better still, don't be afraid to ask for help from people who are willing to do the jobs around the house, so that you can look after yourself and your baby.

Breastfeeding is a partnership, and it takes time for you and your baby to learn from each other, to get established as a couple, and settle, but after some weeks, you will suddenly realise that it seems like the most natural thing in the world (which it is).

BREASTFEEDING AND FOOD ALLERGY

Mothers frequently ask whether good nutrition during pregnancy and lactation helps prevent allergies, both in the mother and in the child in later years. Food allergy and food intolerance appear to be getting more common, and it is probable that the poor eating habits of teenagers is partly responsible for that.

Starting at the earliest moment, straight after birth, the best nutrition of all is that provided by mother's milk. This wonderful food also provides immunological protection for the baby and activates mother/baby love. Mother's breast alters the composition of its milk from day to day and minute to minute, so as ideally to suit baby's changing needs. The breast is a complex biochemical and immunological factory, constantly sampling mother's bloodstream and passing on to the baby tiny doses of food molecules that mother herself has been eating. To these food molecules the breast adds a healthy dose of antibodies against those food molecules, thus preparing the baby gently for the day when she will start on those foods herself.

Problems can arise, though, when the baby is allergic to one of these foodstuffs. This is more likely if one or both parents are themselves allergic, but can also strike "out of the blue" in a baby with perfectly healthy parents. The result is a baby who is "allergic to her own mother's milk!" - at least some of the time. She's not really allergic to mother's milk, only to the traces of that particular food that her mother has ingested. If the baby starts shrieking inconsolably the day after the mother ate prawns, for example, you don't have to look far to make the connection. Of course, babies shriek for all sorts of other reasons too, and it may be impossible to be sure. If the baby is allergic to a food the mother takes every day, she may well shriek every day (and night), probably because her tummy hurts all the time. Severely allergic babies may have chronic diarrhoea and fail to grow properly.

Sadly, the commonest foodstuff to cause allergies is cow's milk and its various products, and this of course is one of those foodstuffs that most mothers have every day, in one form or another. So if a baby cries all the time when being breastfed, the mother would be well advised to try the experiment of omitting milk herself for a few days. If baby quietens down, mother will have to continue avoiding milk, and will need to find other sources of calcium and protein until after weaning. If milk avoidance doesn't help, it may be some other food antigen, such as fish, citrus, coffee or soya, and it will be a good idea for mother to try the effect of avoiding those also. If that also fails to improve matters, guesswork has failed, and the last resort will be a GP referral to the Regional Immunology Laboratory, where her milk can be sampled for food antigens. Certainly it is NOT a good idea to abandon breastfeeding without at least trying!

Whether breastfeeding protects the baby against developing allergies in later life is still controversial (breastfeeding is a particularly emotive subject!) but in general the positive evidence is mounting and getting stronger, and can now be accepted as the truth, especially when one or both parents are also allergic. The best is exclusive breastfeeding, with baby having nothing at all apart from that, not even a drink of water. (Don't worry about baby becoming dehydrated. On very hot days, babies regulate their intake, if allowed to, so as to suck more of the foremilk, which is much more watery than the fatty aftermilk, and they are at no risk).

But if baby has had some other feed apart from mother's milk, don't despair; any breast milk is better than none. The entire anti-allergic effect of breastfeeding is likely to be lost if the mother smokes. (Even the father smoking will encourage allergies to some extent).

The commonest foods to cause allergic reactions are (in approximate order of frequency):

1. Milk and its products

2. Wheat

3. Food preservatives, colourings and other additives

4. Fish

5. Soya

6. Citrus

7. Coffee

Artificial sweeteners are also somewhat worrisome; theoretically it would not be suprising if they caused allergic reactions, but in practice reports of clinical reactions are still few. After those common food allergens, the list goes on to a huge variety of other foods, all of which cause allergy sometimes but not so frequently. Some mothers, if they themselves had allergies, are advised to avoid the commonest allergens during pregnancy and lactation, whether or not they have reactions to them. They are also advised not to wean their babies onto milk, wheat, etc but onto "safe" foods like lamb or potato. I think this advice is both too lenient and too restrictive. On the one hand, there is no such thing as a "safe food" in allergy; who is to say that this particular baby might not be allergic to lamb and potato? On the other hand, by avoiding milk and wheat until long after weaning, we may be denying the baby their goodness while also losing the safety factor given by early breastfeeding.

Weaning, in my view, should begin at whatever age the baby starts to reach out for the foods on mother's plate, and the baby should be offered exactly those foods that she was herself consuming while lactating, suitably mashed, puréed or as finger foods. There is no point in using prepared tins and jars of special "baby-food" - why should they suit baby any better than anything else? Provided mother has been eating bread etc frequently during lactation, with no obvious problem, baby should be given bread as well, preferably wholemeal, so as to get accustomed to it and derive its full goodness while still protected by his mother's milk. If in spite of that there are still allergic reactions, they will soon become obvious and only then will it be necessary to avoid that food.

Be on the watch, during the toddler years, for the development of food addictions. This seems a strange, even paradoxical concept, but it happens. Certain foods contain peptides (partially digested proteins) which exert an effect rather like a small dose of morphine - hence the name exorphins. This effect cannot work in a child with a healthy strong digestion, only in one whose digestive system does not completely digest protein, but there is no easy way of telling this in advance. If you see a child gradually becoming more faddy and picky about his food, watch to see what it is he really likes, and will eat a lot of. There's almost always something. Once again, the commonest food addictants are milk, wheat and caffeine. The classic picture is of a child who likes nothing but breakfast cereal with milk, bread, chocolate and cola drinks. Offer him meat and green vegetables and he'll suddenly lose all appetite, even though he strongly maintains he is hungry. This is food addiction. It is not a true allergy, but is likely to lead to one in years to come (besides being nutritionally unbalanced). It can be nipped in the bud, if spotted early, by keeping the diet varied, so that no food item becomes a daily habit.

INTRODUCING SOLID FOODS

Your baby will continue to benefit from being freely breastfed during the months when he is experimenting with solid food. The information that follows will help you to make this gradual change a happy one for both of you.

WHEN

Your breast milk is the perfect first food. Usually there is no need to add any other food until about the middle of the first year of life at the earliest. In certain cases a doctor might have a medical reason to advise you to start solids earlier. Otherwise there are good reasons to wait - to keep up your milk supply, and to lessen the likelihood of allergic reactions to foods.

A baby may seem ready for solids earlier than this, but other reasons may be the cause. Most babies have a growth spurt and demand more milk around three months. As in the early days of breastfeeding, the way to make more milk is to feed more often, continuing to let the baby decide when the feed is finished. Don't leave long gaps between feeds. At four months many babies like to be involved at mealtimes in a sociable way - a spoon to play with is often enough at this stage.

At around six months of age, a baby is usually interested in and ready to try solid food. Let your baby be the guide. Some babies are ready before others. There is no need to introduce solids just because other babies of the same age are eating them. He is probably able to sit up on his own now. He can usually reach out for an object, hold it, and carry it to his mouth. He may try to grab food on its way to his mother's mouth from her plate. His tongue will no longer automatically push out anything that is put in his mouth.

He may be wanting more frequent breastfeeds. However there may be other reasons for this, even at six months. He may be teething, poorly, or reacting to some kind of stress.

How to tell if your baby is ready for solids

Signs that a baby is ready include:

- Sitting up unaided
- Head erect
- "Extrusion" reflex (spitting/gagging) disappears
- Good hand to mouth co-ordination
- Rhythmic biting movements
- Erupting first teeth
- Gut mature, enabling proper digestion of food.

Most of these signs are showing in a baby around the middle of the first year. At this time the baby is able to pick up suitable foods and try them for himself. So waiting till then, knowing breastmilk is supplying all your baby's nutritional needs, means there is less need to purée everything to a mush! Many LLL mothers have introduced their babies to healthy everyday food from the family table without ever preparing a special purée, or opening a tin, bottle or packet of commercial baby food.

HOW

A very hungry baby won't want to try anything new. For the first weeks breastfeed your baby first and then offer some solids. Don't be afraid to put him back to the breast afterwards, too. Breastmilk is the most important food in your baby's diet for the first year, as well as providing a drink if he is thirsty.

One at a time

Introduce new foods one at a time, once or twice a day. See the chart for suggestions of some good first foods. Try to allow a week between each new food. An allergic reaction is less likely at six months than earlier, but it is still possible. If a food causes a reaction - such as wheezing, a rash, a runny nose, or a sore bottom - cut out that food for a week, then try again. If it has the same effect two or three times, leave it out for at least six months. The reaction could be a temporary food intolerance due to your baby's immature digestive system.

If there is no history of allergy in the family, then mixing foods in a meal after a few weeks is good, as fruits and vegetables high in vitamin C will help increase the iron available to the baby from other foods.

Let him feed himself

Start with a quarter of a teaspoonful of the new food, increasing the amount little by little each day until after a week he is getting as much of it as he wants.

Put this small amount of food in front of him and let him feed himself. Show him with your smile that this is something he will like. You can help casually with a spoon from time to time if he seems to need help (and doesn't object) but don't take over entirely. This is his project. When he grabs for the spoon, let him have it and pick up another for yourself. Finger foods help him gain co-ordination and muscle control.

A baby should never be left to eat alone. Always stay with him in case he chokes.

Plan to enjoy a little mess

A little mess is all part of the game. If you plan for it, you won't be so irritated and can clean up more easily. Newspapers or a plastic table cloth on the floor and around the highchair are a great help. If your baby gets messy - and he will if he is really enjoying himself - you can always bath him later on. What a good excuse for a cuddle in a soft towel!

Not interested in food?

If your baby isn't interested the first few times, just forget the whole project for another week or so and then try again. Sometimes a baby isn't really interested in solids until eight or nine months, or even longer. You may also find that your baby's appetite for solids varies from week to week. Don't worry. Your milk will continue to nourish him until he is ready to accept other food as long as you continue to breastfeed as frequently as your baby wants and until he has finished. If your baby is active, gaining well, and remaining healthy there should be no need for any milk other than breast milk, vitamin or iron supplements. Just continue to offer some food every now and then and always be cheerful when you do. If he refuses food he is not rejecting you. He is just telling you that he is not ready for this stage yet.

If your baby isn't eating very much and continues to rely almost entirely on breastmilk from six months to a year, as many babies do without ill effects, do remember to eat a well-balanced diet yourself with plenty of fresh food. Remember, too, to feed your baby as often as he wants. If weight gain remains a worry, the addition of a little olive oil to whatever he will eat, will boost the calories. You may find that your baby is not interested in solid foods after he has been eating them for a while. This may mean that he is unwell or possibly cutting a tooth. He will let you know that he needs plenty of breastfeeding until he is feeling better and ready to return to solids.

WHAT
Fresh, natural, healthy
Many mothers these days are changing over to fresh, natural foods, which are good for all the family. The closer a food is to its natural state, the better it is nutritionally. Fresh fruit has more food value than tinned. Fresh vegetables are best, especially if not overcooked. If you can't get really fresh vegetables then frozen vegetables do retain most of their nutrient value. Whole grains are good, but because of the greater bulk, babies may fill up before they get enough calories.

The best drink for babies is still breastmilk, next best is plain water. Fruit drinks, soft drinks, tea, coffee, are all full of sugar or other substances which are nutritionally bad for babies.

Homemade food
Since your breastmilk contains traces of whatever you have been eating, your baby has already been introduced to those foods via your milk. It makes sense to start your baby off with things that you yourself often have, provided he shows no signs of reacting to them. You can add items of family food to your baby's diet one by one. Choose things from the family meal which are suitable for your baby. Take out the baby's portion and mash it, or give him a piece in his fingers. A variety of natural foods will give him all the nourishment he needs in addition to your breastmilk. Soon he will be eating the same healthy diet as the rest of the family.

Value for money
Convenience foods have a lot done to them and you pay for every stage. You pay for the packet, jar, or tin, too. Your baby will thrive if you never buy a single jar. Some commercial baby foods contain thickening agents, salt, sugar, or other sweeteners which can be dangerous for babies.

It makes sense to choose fresh food for all the family - you can spend your money on delicious food, not on packaging, fillers, and additives.

Long before someone discovered that putting strained food into jars and selling them as baby food was very profitable, babies thrived on fresh, natural foods.

WHAT TO AVOID
Sugar and artifical sweeteners
Sweetness comes in many forms. The commonest type of sugar we add to our food is sucrose (refined from cane or sugar beet). This is not essential for anyone and contributes to obesity and tooth decay, which could affect your child for the rest of his life. If glucose, dextrose, or molasses (other forms of sugar) are added to your baby's food, they have all the same disadvantages as sucrose. Fruit sugar (fructose) is present in many fruits and vegetables. Because it is combined with fibre, your child is unlikely to get too much of it. Milk sugar (lactose) is what makes breastmilk sweet. It is just the right kind and in just the right proportion for babies.

Foods with added sugar or sweeteners can displace healthy foods from the diet. Babies don't need any added sugar. Processed foods which may have added sugar include: sweets, puddings, jelly, cakes, biscuits, teething biscuits, tinned fruit, soft drinks and fruit drinks. Many of these may also have artificial sweeteners which are not good for babies.

Honey is almost pure sugar. It should never be given to babies under a year old, as it may contain spores of botulism - a serious infection.

Also leave out teething biscuits. They are made from refined carbohydrates with little food value and baby doesn't need them. He can teethe very nicely without them, using anything hard and safe to chew on.

Mustard, ketchup, horseradish sauce, yeast extract, salted crisps and so on are high in salt and/or sugar and are therefore not recommended for babies.

Tea and coffee, even decaffeinated varieties, contain substances that make the iron in food unusable by the body so are not suitable drinks for babies and young children.

MORE PLEASE

Give your baby more of any food as he indicates that he wants it. When he doesn't want more, stop. Don't ever coax, cajole, wheedle, or force him to eat. If he is suspicious of a new food, you can mix it with a food that has already been introduced. If he doesn't want a certain food, try something else. Babies who are allowed free choice of only good, nutritious food will balance their own diets.

AVOIDING ALLERGY

Remember that most babies are not allergic. If allergies are not common in your family and your baby does not show signs of reacting to the foods most likely to cause allergy, then these foods can form a useful part of a weaning diet.

Total breastfeeding for at least six months gives a baby the best chance of avoiding allergy. Is there anyone in your family who suffers from eczema, asthma, hay-fever, hyperactivity, or other allergic illness? If so, you will probably need to delay solids for at least six months, but be guided by the baby, and to be more careful about which foods to introduce before your baby's first birthday.

These are the foods most likely to cause allergy:

Cows' milk and dairy products - the commonest cause of food allergy in babies. Freely breastfed babies are getting all the milk they need from mum. You may wish to avoid cows' milk products altogether whilst cows' milk can be a useful part of a mixed diet many children grow to be very healthy without it.

Wheat, rye, barley, oats - delay giving any foods based on these cereals until after six months.

Egg-white, fish (including shellfish), goats' milk, soya products, tomatoes, berries, nuts, citrus fruits, strawberries, chocolate. Many parents who have allergies prefer to delay introduction of these foods for a least a year or more.

Some colourings added to processed food to improve the appearance may be associated with allergy.

Your doctor should be able to help you with any difficulties involving food allergy.

AS LONG AS YOU LIKE

Soon, your baby will be eating the same food as you, but he may still need to breastfeed. Feeding him yourself is a wonderful way to mother a crawling and toddling baby, to give him comfort, and to show him love. Breastmilk is nourishing for older babies too. It still contains antibodies to help him fight off illness, and is a valuable resource when he is poorly. More and more mothers are finding that breastfeeding can go on for as long as they and their babies like.

FIRST FOODS

FOOD	HOW TO SERVE	COMMENTS
Some good starting foods:		
Rice	Mashed boiled rice or ground rice cooked with water or breast milk	
Ripe banana	Mashed, or baby holds a piece, or mix with breast milk.	Smooth consistency, tasty.
Potato, sweet potato, yam	Bake whole or steam. Remove peel. Mash small amounts with cooking water or breast milk.	Good source of vitamin C. Most babies love the taste and consistency.
Avocado	Mashed or give a piece to hold.	Contains vitamins and oil.
Chicken, poultry, other meats	Small slivers of stewed meat mashed with a fork and moistened with meat juices.	Meat is no more essential to a baby than to an adult.
Liver, kidney, etc.	Slice thinly and shallow fry. Cool, chop or mash. Freeze baby-size portions of meat (e.g. in ice-cube tray). Defrost and steam for a quick meal when family meal is not suitable for baby.	Very high in iron. Consistency is just right if not overcooked.
Later ...		
Fresh fruits: Apple, pear, peach, apricot, plum, melon	Peel, core and grate or scrape with a spoon OR Wedge of peeled cored fruit for baby to hold.	All fruits contains essential vitamins and minerals.
Vegetables	Steam and mash. Your child could gnaw on a large chunk of raw carrot or celery, but care should be taken with any raw vegetable given to a child under three years because of the danger of choking or inhaling a small piece so never leave the child alone with raw vegetables. Rich in vitamins.	
Mushrooms	Stir-fry	Excellent scource of protein, minerals and vitamins.

FOOD	HOW TO SERVE	COMMENTS
Foods marked * often trigger allergy. Wait until your baby is well past 6 months to introduce these foods, and then use only in small amounts. If anyone in your family has allergies, you may want to avoid these foods till your baby is past a year old. See Avoiding Allergy page 8.		
Lentils	No need to soak. Simmer for about 25 minutes.	Good source of protein, high in calcium and some iron. Red are best for babies.
Beans	Soak overnight. Check cooking times. A pressure cooker reduces times by two-thirds.	Delay soya beans*. Cook all beans thoroughly.
Wholemeal bread*	Give a piece dried or toasted for baby to hold. Spread with butter or marge to reduce risk of choking on crumbs.	Handy snack. Better value than rusks which may contain egg, sugar, sweeteners and preservatives and cost more.
Wholegrain cereals*	Cook with water - no sugar, sweetener or salt.	Better value than commercial baby cereals.
Pasta*	Cook with water.	
Other ripe fruit	Remove pips, seeds, peel.	After 8 months (some fruits cause a rash in some children if given too early).
Citrus fruit*	Peel, chop, remove seeds.	Some children react badly, especially to orange juice.
Dried fruits		Though rich in minerals, stick between teeth, so contribute to tooth decay. Clean teeth thoroughly.
Nuts*	Should never be given whole to young children. Peanuts especially should be avoided, as a piece of peanut is very dangerous when inhaled by a small child. Well after 6 months other nuts may be given ground up or liquidized.	
Fish*	Steam or bake.	
Fromage frais, yoghurt, cottage cheese, other dairy products*	Add fresh fruit to natural yoghurt.	Avoid artificial flavours, colours, sugar and sweeteners.
Cheese*	Grate or slice	
Drinks: Water Unsweetened pure fruit and vegetable juices Cow's milk	IT IS NOT NECESSARY TO GIVE DRINKS IN A BOTTLE. Boil and cool. Small amount in unbreakable cup. Dilute well to lessen danger of tooth decay. Small amount in cup. Cow's milk is one of the commonest triggers of food allergy. A baby who gets plenty of milk from mum does not need any cow's milk. Most powdered baby milks and follow-on milks are made from cow's milk.	When he wants a drink with food. Read labels: avoid sugar and additives.
Spreads: Peanut butter* tahini (sesame seed paste), hazelnut butter, sunflower spread.	Spread on wholemeal cracker or rice cake (baby could choke on a spoonful).	Good high calorie food for picky eaters. Lots of protein and calcium.

ADAPTING FAMILY MEALS FOR BABIES, TODDLERS AND YOUNG CHILDREN

By breastfeeding their babies for as long as they show the need, and introducing other foods gradually, thousands of mothers have found it possible to enable their children to progress from the breast to independent eating at the family table without ever using a bottle or commercial baby food (just as they must have done since time immemorial). So how is it done? Firstly, with faith that breastmilk will continue to provide most of the baby's nutritional needs. Then, gradually, trusting your young child to let you know their needs. When the baby shows signs of being ready to try other foods (for example by trying to grab the food from your plate) you can slowly introduce foods from your family meals. Cooked potatoes, rice and pasta are all easy to serve. A teaspoonful is all that is needed at first, mashed up with a fork, or in pieces that can be held in the hand. A little sauce from your casserole, or soup, can be given in a bowl, to dip rice cakes, bread sticks or toast into.

There are no special "baby" meals in this book. Just let your toddlers try what is on offer, make allowances for their genuine dislikes, and give them the pleasure of real food from the very beginning.

INVOLVING CHILDREN IN THE KITCHEN

Letting your children help in the kitchen is often a good way to interest them in food. But if they have been trying and tasting, don't be surprised if they don't want to eat much at the table!

Preparing food for the family is something even the youngest can help with. A baby watching from a side or back sling is seeing the shapes, colour, and action of real life, and experiencing their sounds and smells. A toddler can wash salads and tear them up, or help scrub potatoes (put a bowl of water on the kitchen floor for this), stir dried fruit into cake mixtures, model pastry and dough shapes, or cut them out, mix muesli, make collages with dried beans and pasta. An older child can cut out paper cake tin linings, decorate cakes or biscuits, shell peas and beans, make interesting designs on pizzas, and begin to cook for themselves, under supervision. Growing things may arouse interest and encourage a child to try something they would never otherwise eat. (It worked with lettuce in our family). In this way, your children will meet maths (counting, weighing, measuring), chemistry (what happens when things are mixed and subjected to heat or cold), the earth sciences (growing things), reading (words on labels), motor skills (mixing, tearing, modelling), creativity (patterns, shapes, colours, design, collages). All this and learning about good food too.

GUIDELINES FOR A BALANCED, HEALTHY DIET

These days, we are bombarded with advice about healthy eating from newspapers, television and radio. Sometimes this advice may increase our anxiety about a particular nutrient. "Am I getting enough iron in my diet? If I'm not, what effect will this have on my health?"

What you eat is important and it does influence your health. But eating should be an enjoyable part of life; something you enjoy doing with your family and friends, not a continual source of worry. So here are some useful guidelines.

No single food is essential or can supply all the nutrients you need. Don't worry about those people who throw up their hands in horror when your toddler refuses to eat cabbage or roast beef. The nutrients found in one food can also be found in many others so...

The more variety the better

Eating a wide range of foods gives you more chance of getting all the nutrients you need. You will also be able to tailor your diet to your budget, tastes and what is locally available. A varied diet is also more fun than a restricted one.

The Good News: advice on healthy eating doesn't have to be just a list of what to avoid or cut down on. There are some foods which nutritionists want you to eat more of and enjoy!

Starchy foods

Once upon a time we were advised to reduce the amount of starchy foods (such as bread and potatoes) we ate, especially if we wanted to lose weight. Starchy foods are now known to be good for you, especially if you choose the whole grain or wholemeal varieties. These have more dietary fibre than the refined or white varieties. Dietary fibre may protect you against bowel cancer and it certainly prevents constipation. So a healthy diet should contain lots of wholemeal bread, wholemeal pastas, brown rice, wholemeal breakfast cereals as well as starchy vegetables such as potatoes and baked beans, lentils and other pulses, wherever possible.

Fruit and vegetables

The World Health Organization recommend that we all eat five servings of fruit and vegetables a day (about 400 g or 14 oz). They contain vitamins, notably the antioxidants A, C and E, and minerals which are an important part of a healthy diet, some dietary fibre and are also low in calories which is important if you are trying to lose weight. They also contain nutrients which may be important in preventing some cancers and improve resistance to infection. Frozen vegetables are as good as fresh ones and fruit and vegetable juices are also important. It is cheapest to eat whatever is in season; satsumas at Christmas, peaches in the summer, courgettes and aubergines in the early autumn. Stir fry, salads, chopped vegetables with dips and vegetable soups are all ways of making vegetables more appealing to your family.

Calcium

This is the mineral which gives bones and teeth their strength. Growing children need calcium to enable their bones to grow. Your skeleton is constantly being remodelled and in adults the entire skeleton is replaced every 7-10 years. People over 65 years of age may be less able to absorb calcium from their food. Women who have passed the menopause are less able to replace the calcium which is naturally lost from their bones. Older people, especially women, are at risk from a condition called osteoporosis, where their bones contain less calcium than they should and are weak and fracture easily. It is therefore important to eat enough calcium in childhood and early adulthood to make sure that your bones are as strong as possible before age and hormonal changes weaken them.

   Milk and dairy products supply more than half the calcium in an average diet. For people who do not like milk or who are allergic to it, a list of calcium exchanges is helpful. This shows the calcium contents of foods compared with 1/3 pint of milk. Whole milk, semi-skimmed and skimmed milk are all roughly equal in calcium content.

		Calcium Exchange
1 oz (28 g)	cheddar cheese	1
5 oz (140 g)	yoghurt	1
3 oz (84 g)	cottage cheese	1/4
4 oz (112 g)	ice cream	1/2
2 oz (56 g)	sardines with bones	1
2 large (60 g)	slices bread white or brown	1/4
2 large (60 g)	slices wholemeal bread	1/8
4 oz (112 g)	spring greens cooked	1/4
4 oz (112 g)	broccoli cooked	1/8
4 oz (112 g)	baked beans	1/4
2 oz (56 g)	peanuts plain	1/8
2 oz (56 g)	apricots dried	1/4
1	large orange	1/4
3 oz (84 g)	shelled prawns	1/2

A breastfeeding woman needs to eat 5 calcium exchanges per day. She could do this by eating 84 g shelled prawns, 6 slices brown bread, 400 ml milk, 1 yoghurt, 1 orange, 112 g baked beans and 56 g dried apricots.

Protein
Many articles and books on healthy eating emphasise the importance of protein and 'protein foods' such as meat, fish, eggs, milk, cheese etc. Although children need protein for growth and repair of worn out cells, adults need it for repair only. Most British diets supply more than adequate amounts of protein and most people would not need to worry about their daily intake.

Vegetarian diets: Many people following a vegetarian diet worry about the lack of protein. However, with the exception of fruit, protein is present in most foods of plant origin. But, unlike animal foods, plant foods do not always contain all the essential amino acids, or in the proportions we need. Combining grains, cereals and nuts with dairy products and eggs or soya products will provide all the necessary amino acids. This does not have to be done consciously and it is not necessary to have an exact balance of amino acids at every meal; many meals naturally contain a balance of protein foods. Examples are beans on toast, rice and peas, or cereal and milk.

Iron

Is needed to prevent anaemia. Infants, toddlers, adolescents, pregnant and menstruating women and some elderly people may be at risk from this condition. Iron-containing foods are:

- red meat
- egg yolk
- breakfast cereal (some have iron added)
- whole-wheat bread, pasta, brown rice
- dried fruit, especially apricots and raisins
- nuts
- sesame seeds, tahini, hummus
- broccoli and other dark green leafy vegetables

The absorption of iron from all these foods is aided by vitamin C found in citrus fruit and fruit juices.

Now the bad news...

In this country we eat more fatty foods, salt and sugar than is good for us. We need to reduce the amounts we eat of these foods, in order to be healthier.

A high fat diet is one of the factors which can increase your risk of heart disease and some cancers. It can also make you overweight. Confusingly, there are three types of fat: saturated, polyunsaturated and monounsaturated. Most of the fat in meat is saturated fat, as it is in milk, cheese, butter, lard, some margarines and in cakes, biscuits, chocolate and meat products such as sausages and pies. It is this sort of fat which we need to eat less off. You can do this by:

- trimming fat off meat
- choosing leaner cuts of meat
- removing skin from fish and poultry
- grilling, microwaving, steaming or poaching rather than frying food
- draining off excess fat after cooking
- reducing the amount of pies, sausages, crisps, chocolate and cakes which you eat
- switching to low fat spreads and reduced fat cheeses or cottage cheese
- switching to semi-skimmed or skimmed milk
- reducing the amount of chips you eat; chunky chips contain less fat than thin cut ones

Read the label carefully. If it says 'contains hydrogenated vegetable fat' then this is also saturated fat and you should aim to reduce the amounts of these foods in your diet.

Monounsaturated fat and polyunsaturated fats are not thought to increase your risk of heart disease, but they are still high in calories. So if you are overweight, you need to reduce your intake of all fats, but especially saturated fats. Monounsaturated fats such as olive oil are beneficial because they probably do not raise blood cholesterol.

Salt
We only need about half a teaspoonful a day but on average we eat two and a half teaspoonfuls. Processed foods contain a lot of salt and we often add it to foods during cooking and at the table. People also get used to the taste of salty foods and perhaps they need to add more and more salt to get the same effect.

You can reduce your salt intake by:
- gradually reduce the amount of salt you add at the table and in cooking
- experimenting with other flavourings e.g. lemon, pepper, herbs and spices
- eating less processed and preserved meats e.g. bacon, ham, salami
- eating less salted snacks e.g. crisps, salted nuts, salted biscuits

Sugar
This supplies energy but no useful nutrients. In Britain we buy 44 kg of sugar per person per year on average. Some of this is hidden in foods such as cakes, biscuits, ice cream and even savoury tinned foods such as vegetables. In these foods, sugar may be eaten without you realizing it. Sugar causes tooth decay and contributes to excess body weight. You can also become so used to sweet tasting food that you cannot imagine cutting down your consumption of sugar. Glucose, dextrose, fructose and maltose are all forms of sugar.

You can reduce your sugar intake by:
- limiting sugary foods to the end of meal times only
- gradually reducing the amount of sugar you add to drinks such as tea and coffee
- choosing low calorie or reduced sugar/sugar free versions of soft drinks and desserts e.g. sugar free fizzy drinks, reduced sugar dessert whips
- drinking pure, unsweetened fruit juice diluted with water
- chosing 'no sugar added' versions of tinned food
- avoiding sugar coated breakfast cereals
- eating fresh fruit without sugar

Eating During Pregnancy
In order to reduce the risk of having a baby with Spina Bifida (a deformity of the spine) pregnant women are advised to have sufficient folic acid in their diets, especially during the first 12 weeks of pregnancy when the baby's spine is developing. If you are planning a pregnancy, you should make sure that your diet is rich in folic acid. This is found in frozen peas, broccoli, spinach, green beans, sprouts, potatoes, oranges and orange juice, bread, some breakfast cereals, baked beans, milk and yoghurt, yeast and meat extract. Folic acid is destroyed by prolonged cooking. Current official advice is to take a folic acid supplement from before you conceive until the 12 th week of your pregnancy. These are available from a chemist or health food shop. If you are taking any other medicines at all, you should ask your doctor for advice about this.

General food safety guidelines

- Use fresh food.
- Wash hands before handling and preparing food.
- Wash all salads, vegetables and fruit in cold water, even those from the supermarket which look clean.
- Keep food in a fridge or cool dark larder.
- Biscuits, cakes and other baked goods should be kept in an airtight container.
- Raw poultry and meat may contain bacteria which could cause food poisoning. Thorough cooking at a high temperature destroys these bacteria.
- Raw meat and poultry can contaminate other foods in the kitchen or refrigerator if their juices are allowed to drip onto foods which will not be cooked before being eaten, or if a knife or chopping board is used to prepare raw meat and not washed before being used to prepare a salad for instance. So try to use separate boards for cooked and raw meat and vegetables; or wash thoroughly between uses.
- Keep fridges at 5 degrees celcius or below and freezers at -18 degrees celcius or below.
- In the fridge: keep cooked and raw meat separated, on different shelves and in different containers; keep left-overs covered and use within 24-48 hours; regularly wipe out with a sterilising solution.
- In the freezer: freeze food fast, keep it below -18 degrees celcius; check commercial foods for maximum keeping times; check contents regularly and use up old stock; do not refreeze food which has been thawed (unless it has been cooked first).
- In the larder: vegetables may be kept in vegetable racks, but should be used quickly, and checked for bruising, mould or sprouting; dried goods in packets should be kept in airtight containers; once opened, tinned goods should be transferred to airtight containers and kept in the fridge; keep shelves clean of grease, flour, crumbs etc.
- Reheating food: All food which is being reheated should be piping hot all the way through. (This is particularly important for the use of microwave ovens, when sometimes food can be hot on the edges, but still cold in the centre, or have hot spots).
- Frozen food should be thawed slowly but completely before cooking. This applies especially to raw meat such as turkey, chickens, joints. However small items and commercial items such as fish fingers, frozen chips and vegetables can be cooked from frozen.

Further information on food safety is available from Environmental Health Offices.

Safety During Pregnancy

Some foods may contain micro organisms which could make you or your baby extremely ill. The British government gives the following advice specifically about food for pregnant women, babies and young children:

- Whilst pregnant, you should avoid soft ripened cheese such as Brie, Camembert, or those with blue veins, and avoid pâté since the Listeria bacterium may be found in them.
- Hard cheese, cottage cheese, cheese spread and processed cheese are all safe.
- Cooked chilled meats and cooked poultry bought from the chill cabinet may also contain Listeria and should be avoided. In all cases anyway bought cooked chilled meals should be reheated until piping hot.

- Pregnant women and young children should only eat eggs which have been cooked until the white and the yolk are solid. The Salmonella bacterium is particularly associated with poultry and eggs so everyone is advised to avoid raw eggs and dishes containing uncooked eggs. Salmonella food poisoning may not directly harm the unborn child, but the sickness and diarrhoea it causes are extremely unpleasant.

- Foods containing pasteurised eggs e.g. some types of mayonnaise, are safe.

If you do suffer from food poisoning, it is advisable to contact your local Environmental Health Officer. Goat's milk, raw meat and the soil around vegetables may all contain Toxoplasma, which can cause still births and other damage to the unborn baby. Goat's milk must be pasteurised, sterilised or UHT (ultra heat treated) and vegetables must be thoroughly washed to remove any soil from them.

Food additives
These are used to make food look better and last longer on the shelf, or to improve the flavour. However some additives may cause allergic reactions in a few children and adults. If this happens to someone in your family, you need to read labels carefully to find out which additives to avoid.

Peanut warning
Asthma and eczema are sometimes triggered by food allergies, one of the most common culprits being peanuts which in very rare cases can cause a severe allergic reaction, called anaphylactic shock. Their size and shape also make them a potential choking hazard. Peanut butter is a popular and nutritious spread, but in view of an increase in the number of cases of peanut allergy in recent years, some experts are of the opinion that products containing peanut or peanut oil should not be introduced to a child's diet before the age of four.

THE HEALTHY WHOLEFOOD STORE CUPBOARD

A note on ingredients
Some store cupboard standbys are essential. The most popular are:

Tinned tomatoes: very handy for sauces and casseroles. Whole peeled plum tomatoes are usually cheapest and can easily be broken down with a spoon or in a blender.

Tomato purée: some of the brands in the supermarkets are now made from genetically modified tomatoes so if you are unhappy about the idea of genetically modified foods you should ask or look carefully at the packaging.

Tuna fish: best is tinned in spring water but also available in brine and oil - the latter is useful to tip, oil and all, into a rice or pasta salad.

Tinned beans such as red kidney beans, cannellini beans, chick peas, pinto beans. They are often available without any additions other than salt, and are useful for filling out casseroles and salads.

Tinned fruit in natural juices are good and healthy without the addition of sugar syrup. Handy for pies and tarts.

Other essentials for the recipes in this book include:

Wholemeal flour (plain and self-raising): the best wholemeal flour is stoneground, this means it has been milled by stone rather than steel rollers. You may see 100% or 85% wholemeal available. 100% contains all the valuable vitamins and minerals which are found in the outer husk and central wheatgerm. The 85% flour is milled so that most of the bran is removed reducing it by 15%. This is therefore finer and paler than 100% flour.

Soya flour is a pale, fine flour made from ground soya bean. It is a very rich source of protein, twice that of wheat flour, and is usually mixed with other flours to give additional food value. It is useful for gluten-free diets.

Easy blend dried yeast usually sold in sachets or tins. This is used instead of fresh yeast. Use half the weight of dried yeast if a recipe indicates fresh yeast - so use 15 g (1/2 oz) instead of 25 g (1 oz) fresh.

Oatmeal and oatflakes: higher in protein than other grains, oatmeal is rolled or cut whole grain and is available in fine, medium or coarse.

Long-grain brown rice is the wholegrain with only the inedible outer husk removed, leaving bran-covered rice which is brownish in colour with a nutty flavour and a chewy texture. When the bran is removed it gives white or polished rice. Brown rice takes longer to cook than white rice and the covering of bran means it can go rancid so keep it for no longer than six months. Basmati rice is one of the most popular and easy to cook varieties of long grain.

Lentils (green and red) don't need soaking before cooking, so they are useful for quick soups, salads and stews. The red lentils usually cook down to a purée whereas green lentils hold their shape. Lentils have fair quantities of calcium and vitamins A and B and are a good source of iron as well as high protein content.

Dried beans: haricot, soya, flageolet, red kidney beans are all rich in iron, phosphorous, calcium and protein. Dried beans need to be soaked for several hours or overnight. Red kidney beans have been found to contain toxins called lectins but these are destroyed if the beans are boiled on a high heat for 10 minutes. People often complain of gasiness after eating beans. This is caused by complex sugars called oligosaccharides, which because they are indigestible by normal stomach enzymes proceed to ferment, the result of which is gas. Some people say a pinch of bicarbonate of soda in the cooking water helps, others that if you eat beans regularly your stomach gets accustomed to them. It's best not to add salt to the cooking water as it has a tendency to toughen the beans and prevent them cooking, so add when the beans are cooked.

Bean sprouts: you can grow your own bean sprouts at home. They are a valuable source of vitamins as well as being fun for children to produce. You can make salads, sandwiches or stir- fries with them depending on which beans you choose to sprout. Mung beans are the most commonly used beans for producing bean sprouts but you can use green or brown lentils, alfalfa, chick peas, fenugreek and soybeans.

The basic technique is very simple. Soak the seeds or beans overnight in warm water. Then drain them and keep for 3-5 days where they are warm, moist and dark. You can buy a kit for sprouting in wholefood shops but it's easy to improvise with a jar covered with muslin or cheesecloth. The beans should be rinsed and drained two or three times a day and kept somewhere warm at 21°C (70°F). If they get too wet or warm they will go mouldy.

Grains such as pot or pearl barley, bulgar wheat, couscous, buckwheat, quinoa, wheat berries, millet. These are all edible seeds from the grass family and are an inexpensive source of protein. They also have more carbohydrates than any other food. They do not need soaking before cooking. Pot barley has only the outer husk removed and is the most nutritious form of the grain, whereas pearl barley has also had the bran removed and has been steamed and polished. Both are excellent for use in soups and stews.

Bulgar wheat and cracked wheat are both made from whole-grain wheat. Cracked wheat is simply the grain cracked into coarse pieces with the bran and the germ still on the grain. Bulgar has the bran removed and the remaining grain is steamed, dried and cracked.

Quinoa (pronounced keen-wa) is currently regarded as one of the super-grains because of its nutritional profile. Although technically a herb, quinoa resembles unhulled sesame seeds in size, shape and colour and the protein it provides is as high if not higher than a true grain. It also has unusually high quantites of amino acids which are lacking in other grains. It is available from health food shops and it needs thorough rinsing before cooking. When it's cooked it expands to four times its dry volume.

Dried fruits: apricots, prunes, apples, pears, raisins and sultanas are all rich in natural sugar which is called fructose. Also rich in vitamins A and B as well as minerals such as potassium and iron. They make excellent puddings soaked and cooked and served with natural yoghurt (see recipe page 154) or they can be cooked and puréed to make a healthy type of jam. But remember that without preservatives it has a limited life so only make small quantities. Also dried fruits should be well washed before you use them, even if they are organic.

Seeds: sesame, sunflower, pumpkin and alfalfa are useful for sprinkling over salads or mixing in with yoghurt. They are good sources of vitamin B complexes and minerals such as calcium and iron.

Pasta in any varieties of shape and colour including wholemeal and gluten-free kinds.

Oils which are labelled unrefined and cold pressed are the ones to look out for, such as olive oil, sunflower oil, as well as sesame oil which is delicious for flavouring dishes with just a small quantity. Oils are an essential part of a healthy, balanced diet, containing as they do essential fatty acids which are not produced by the body. They contain vitamins A,D,E and K.

Vinegars such as wine vinegar and cider vinegar. Cider vinegar especially is considered to be beneficial to the body's metabolism and is helpful in a number of disorders, especially arthritis.

Carob may be used in any recipe which uses chocolate or cocoa. Carob looks like chocolate but unlike chocolate it is rich in vitamins and contains no refined sugar, and it is beneficial to those wishing to avoid the stimulant effect of caffeine.

Raw brown sugar does not contain any artificial colouring or additives; it is a natural product derived from unrefined cane sugar and produced in its country of origin. You will find demerara, muscovado, and light muscovado. Raw brown sugars have sticky textures because of their natural molasses and can become a solid mass, so they are best stored in airtight containers.

Honey and molasses are good alternative sweeteners to sugar. Honey is sweeter than sucrose and can therefore be used sparingly. It also contains essential fatty acids, minerals and vitamin C.

Concentrated fruit juices are to be found in health food shops and are free from additives, colourings, sugar and artificial sweeteners. These are most suitable to give to children to drink since they are entirely natural. They may seem expensive but they are usually diluted 8 or 10 times with water making them very often cheaper than squashes which appear cheap but are full of sugar and colourings.

Soy sauce: many cheap, commercially produced soy sauces are coloured with caramel and contain preservatives. Tamari is a term you will find on bottles which contain naturally fermented sauce made without the use of chemicals. Some soy sauce is made from a mixture of wheat and soya beans so those with a wheat allergy need to be alert. However there are brands of Tamari soy sauce which are entirely wheat free and are therefore suitable for those on gluten-free diets.

Setting and jelling agents: gelatine is derived from animal carcases and so vegetarians and those concerned about animal welfare and meat sources may want an alternative. The vegetarian alternatives all derive from seaweed, they are Agar-agar, Carrageen and Gelozone and can be found in health food shops.

Salt is a mineral called sodium chloride and is obtained by evaporating sea water, in which case it is sea salt or by mining crystalline deposits in which case it is rock salt. These natural products are rich in minerals.

Dried herbs: it is best to buy these in small quantities and use them fast so that they don't become old and stale.

Dairy products such as milk, cheese and yoghurt are an everyday necessity for some families, but for others they are a potential source of allergy. The nutrients found in dairy products can be obtained from other sources. So there are some recipes which use dairy produce but in most sections of the book there are some which are dairy free.

Bearing in mind our preference for natural, fresh foods, you may wish to seek out organic producers and suppliers of grain, vegetables, eggs, poultry, dairy produce and meat. You may be inspired to grow your own, and that can be very satisfying for you, and instructive for your children. There are some addresses at the back of the book for you to contact for more information.

Mothers of necessity are inventive. The recipes here show it is possible to be creative in using what you have to hand to produce nutritious, simple-to-prepare meals which are tasty and relatively cheap. There are a few that cost more, or are just a bit more complicated but they are worth it for a special occasion. We hope you will enjoy trying them and use them as the springboard for inventing more recipes of your own.

WEIGHTS, MEASURES AND EQUIPMENT

We live in a world of anomalies and confusion, so far as food is concerned. Fresh goods, such as fruit and vegetables and meat which are sold loose are usually priced by the pound (Imperial measure), but in the supermarket, labels give weights in metric measures and decimal places. Thus a pack of mince will be marked for example 0.75 kg. Dry goods, such as flour and rice are also sold in metric quantities, such as 1.5k(kilogram) or 250 grams. We buy milk in pints, but cartons of fruit juice in litres. Recipe books give quantities in metric, with imperial equivalents in brackets, and if they are being sold in America or Australia, Cup measurements are given, but American, Australian and British Cups are all different. And if a recipe calls for 125 g (4 oz) chopped onion, and the only one you have weighs 3oz will it matter ?

Quantities in this book are METRIC with the nearest imperial alternative also given. Use either metric or imperial quantities, do not mix them. The imperial quantities are not exact conversions of the metric quantities but are in correct proportion to the other imperial quantities in the same recipe. But for small amounts (one teaspoon (tsp) up to one tablespoon (tbsp)) spoons are used, because they are more practical. And where it makes sense, numbers rather than weights are given, e.g 1 (medium) onion, rather than 125 g. On the next page are conversion charts, showing typical working equivalents, so that you can work in Imperial or Cups, if you prefer. Just remember that they are not exactly the same, so stick to one kind of measure. The recipes are set out so that there is room for you to write in your own quantities or variations.

In spite of what some cookery experts will tell you, EXACT QUANTITIES AREN'T CRUCIAL. In pastry and some cakes, proportions do matter, but for most of the recipes in this book, 20 g-50 g or an ounce or two either way in the major ingredients, won't make much difference, so long as the general proportions are followed. It is OK to use your own judgement as to the amount of carrots you need in a stew, or beans in a salad, knowing your family's tastes.

As for equipment the most essential tools in the kitchen are nothing more than mixing bowls of various sizes, a chopping board, a very sharp knife, a wooden spoon, a fork, tablespoon and teaspoon, and some pans and casserole dishes for cooking in. Having said that, some electric equipment can be useful: a food processor will grate cabbage or carrots or cheese in a trice, (but creates a lot of washing up); a hand blender is useful for puréeing small amounts for baby; a cordless jug kettle so you can make yourself a cup of tea with one hand; a slow-cooker to prepare a meal early in the day and leave it to look after itself; a microwave oven so you can quickly defrost and cook the meal you forgot to take out of the freezer. Everyone has their own favourite.

Suggested Conversions

Imperial weight	metric working equivalent (as the amounts get bigger so do the differences, so they are rounded up or down)
1 oz	25 g
4 oz	125 g
8 oz	225 g
1 lb	450 g

Metric weight	Imperial working equivalent
25 g	1 oz
125 g	4 oz
225 g	8 oz
250 g	9 oz
750 g	1lb 10oz (or 1½lb)
1 kilogram	2lb 4oz

1 liquid pint = 20 fluid oz = 600 ml   1 litre = 1¾ pints, 500 ml = 18 floz

Cup measures
A measuring cup will hold 125 g (4 oz) of flour, about 180 g (6 oz)
beans or rice, or 200 ml (7 floz or ⅓ pint) liquid.

Spoon measures
One level tablespoon will hold 12 g (½ oz) flour, or 20 g
(3 oz) beans or rice. One rounded tablespoon will hold 25 g (1 oz) flour.

Conventional Oven temperatures (for fan assisted etc, refer to manufacturer's instructions)

	Gas	Electric	
		°F	°C
Low	¼ - 3	225 - 325	110 - 160
Moderate	3 - 5	325 - 375	160 - 190
Hot	5 - 7	375 - 425	190 - 220
Very Hot	7 - 9	425 - 475	220 - 240

Oven temperatures given in the recipes are approximate and usually generalised (e.g. 'moderate').
There are so many different kinds - gas, electric, solid fuel, fan assisted, and microwaves with various
powers and features. You know your own best. Look at the chart and adjust accordingly, within the
given range.

Abbreviations:

tbsp = tablespoon   g = gram   tsp = teaspoon   oz = ounce
dsp = dessertspoon   ml = millilitre   k = kilogram

ABOUT THE RECIPES

Most of the recipes in this book call for fresh ingredients and unrefined wholefoods. In selecting the recipes, priority was given to those which are nutritious, simple to prepare, relatively cheap, and tasty. Most can be adapted easily for babies and toddlers, simply by offering small portions, puréed, mashed or in little pieces that can be picked up.

For your guidance, there is a code with each recipe:

F = Free from egg and dairy products

V = Suitable for vegetarians

Q = Quick (can be prepared and ready to eat within about 30 mins)

Ch = Cheap. Because prices of ingredients vary so much, no price guide is given.
    Cheap meals are those which cost under £2 for the ingredients.

Basics

If you want to use wholewheat flour in any recipe that uses plain white flour you can substitute wholewheat for half of the amount of plain flour.

Bread, Pastry or Batter are so often the staples around which a meal is planned, that basic recipes for these are given here first.

Basic Bread Recipe

The smell of freshly baked bread is something that will linger with your family all their lives. It is the stuff of nostalgia. Bread not only provides breakfast and tea meals, but served with soups or stews can provide the bulk that makes a meal satisfying. Once you have mastered the basic technique, you can experiment by using various combinations of flours, milk instead of water, adding seeds or nuts to the dough, or sprinkling them on top, or adding grated cheese to the dough. Non-wheat flours can be used, but as they contain very little, if any gluten, expect a heavier more solid loaf. Easy blend yeast, which can be bought in sachets, makes the job even easier, just follow the instructions on the packet.

Making your own bread is not such hard work nor as time consuming as people think. The yeast does the hardest part for you! Here is a basic recipe using fresh yeast (often available from small bakers or health food shops).

50 g	fresh yeast	2 oz
3 tsp	sugar	3 tsp
3 tsp	salt	3 tsp
850 ml	warm water or water and milk	1½ pints
1.5 k	flour (any combination of strong white, granary and wholemeal, to suit your family's taste)	3 lb
25 g	oil or margarine	1 oz

GOOD SOURCE

Fibre	Folic acid (T)
Thiamin	Calcium
Riboflavin	Magnesium
Niacin	Iron
Vitamin B6	

Nutrient	Units	per Loaf
Energy	Kcals	2712.68
Protein	g	89.10
Fat	g	23.09
Carbohydrate	g	572.90

Watercress Soup with Leeks and Orange (page 40)

Mix together in a small bowl the yeast and sugar until they form a liquid. Add some of the water and put on one side. In a large bowl, pour the oil or rub the margarine into the flour. Add the yeast mixture, it may have begun to froth by now, and the warm liquid, and bring together to form a dough. Turn onto a floured board and knead until smooth and elastic for about 10 minutes. If the mixture feels too sticky at first, work in some extra flour. Turn the dough into a large container and cover with cling film or a polythene bag. So far, the time and effort is about the same as making scones or pastry, and you haven't been asked to roll it out!

You can now leave the dough standing in the kitchen while you go shopping or to an LLL coffee morning.

When you get home you will find the dough has more than doubled its size. This is called "proving". Turn it back onto a floured board, knock it back to its original size, knead for a couple of minutes, then divide between two or three well greased loaf tins and shape the rest into rolls. Cover again, and leave to prove once more.

You now have about an hour to do something else, be it prepare the rest of the dinner, or play with your toddler, or nurse the baby. When the loaves have doubled their size, bake in a hot oven (gas 8) for 10 minutes, then reduce the heat to gas 7 for a further 20 minutes. (Rolls will take only 15 minutes.) The time-honoured way to test if a loaf is cooked is to tap the bottom. If it sounds hollow, it is done.

Variations: Using easy blend dried yeast. Simply empty the sachet into the flour, add the other dry ingredients,pour in the oil or rub in the margarine, add the warm liquid, then proceed as above. If you are pressed for time prove once only in the loaf tin, and bake when the dough has doubled in size.

If you want to use wholewheat flour in any recipe that uses plain white flour you can substitute wholewheat for half of the amount of plain flour.

Pitta Bread

Cut pitta bread rounds open to form pockets which can be filled with all manner of things - pieces of cold cooked meats, leafy or crunchy salads and cheese, bolognese-style sauces, rice salad, beany stews, or whatever takes your fancy. Pitta bread is ideal for toddlers to hold and eat, as it is less crumbly than slices of ordinary bread. They can also choose for themselves what to put in it.

Using half quantity of the basic bread recipe (page 24), follow the directions for the bread recipe method (page 24) but after the first proving knock the dough back and divide into eight or twelve pieces. Roll each out on a floured board, to make a flat round. Place the rounds in a floured cloth and leave for about 20 minutes.

Preheat a baking sheet in a very hot oven. Remove it from the oven, grease it and place two rounds on it. Return it to the oven and bake the rounds for 4-5 minutes until they begin to puff up. Remove them from the oven, turn them over, then return them to bake for one more minute to brown the second side. Take the breads from the oven, and wrap them in a clean cloth while baking the rest. They are best eaten the same day, preferably still warm.

These freeze well.

GOOD SOURCE

Thiamin

Nutrient	Units	per portn
Energy	Kcals	339.08
Protein	g	11.14
Fat	g	2.89
Carbohydrate	g	71.61

Top: Rainbow Bean Salad (page 80) and Bottom: Refried Bean Dip (page 79)

PIZZA TOPPINGS: the simplest is tomato sauce, grated cheese and fresh chopped oregano or basil. Mozzarella cheese will be more authentic, but if cheddar is what you have in the fridge, that's fine too. Other possibilities are - four cheese pizza (use different cheeses in a wheel pattern); fishy pizza (pieces of cooked smoked fish, or shell fish); veggie pizza (a variety of lightly cooked vegetables such as mushrooms-try different types if you can get them-courgettes, red and green pepper); chopped fresh tomato; pieces of tasty cooked meats such as bacon, sausage, salami.

Nutrient	Units	per base
Energy	Kcals	904.22
Protein	g	29.70
Fat	g	7.70
Carbohydrate	g	190.97

Pizza Base

Young children may like their very own mini pizzas, which they can help to make themselves, choosing and placing the toppings. Or you can make a large pizza in a swiss roll tin, and when it is cold cut it into fingers for toddlers.

Half quantity of the basic bread recipe will make three or four pizza rounds, depending on how big you want them (p24).

Make the dough according to the basic bread recipe. Knock the dough back after the first proving, knead in one tablespoon olive oil and roll out on a floured board to make the pizza rounds. They can be placed on oiled pizza plates, or baking sheets. Leave for about fifteen minutes, or thirty if you like a thick soft pizza base. The basic tomato sauce given on page 44 can be used to spoon over the base.

Serving suggestions: serve with leafy salad as a main meal or lunch.

You can pep up the flavour of the cornbread with half a teaspoon of chilli powder, or a couple of ounces of grated cheese or some finely sliced spring onions.

Cornbread

Sweet, moist cornbread makes a change from yeasted breads and it's so quick and simple to make that it's ideal for children to help mix and bake.

125 g	yellow cornmeal	4 oz
125 g	plain flour	4 oz
125 g	sugar	4 oz
1 tbsp	baking powder	1 tbsp
½ tsp	salt	½ tsp
225 ml	milk	8 floz
2	eggs	2
5 tbsp	melted butter or oil	5 tbsp

Preheat the oven to 400°F (200°C) gas mark 6. Grease 20 cm (8 inch) square baking tin. In a large bowl, stir together the cornmeal, flour, sugar, baking powder and salt. In another bowl beat together the milk, eggs and butter. Stir the liquid into the dry ingredients until just blended. Pour into the prepared pan and bake for about 30 minutes, or until the cornbread is golden brown and firm to the touch. Allow to cool before turning out onto a wire rack.

Nutrient	Units	per loaf
Energy	Kcals	2218.23
Protein	g	44.36
Fat	g	86.60
Carbohydrate	g	336.22

Wholewheat flour has a shorter shelf life than plain flour because of its fat content - it will keep up to six months so buy smaller bags and use it up quickly.

Wholewheat Soda Bread

This simple bread is so quick and easy because it doesn't contain yeast; bicarbonate of soda is used as the raising agent so it can be mixed in no time and goes with any meal.

175 g	plain flour	6 oz
450 g	wholewheat flour	1 lb
2 tbsp	brown sugar	2 tbsp
2 tsp	baking powder	2 tsp
1 tsp	bicarbonate of soda	1 tsp
1 tsp	salt	1 tsp
25 g	butter or margarine	1 oz
425 ml	milk	3/4 pt
2 tbsp	vinegar	2 tbsp

Combine all the dry ingredients in a mixing bowl. Rub in butter until it resembles breadcrumbs. Add the milk and vinegar and mix together to form a soft dough. Turn out onto a lightly floured surface and knead a few times until smooth.

Form the dough into a circle about 7 cm (2¾ inch) thick and place on a greased baking sheet. Cut a large cross about 1cm (½ inch) deep on the top. Bake for one hour at 180°C, 350°F, gas mark 4 or until a skewer inserted in the loaf comes out clean.

Nutrient	Units	per loaf
Energy	Kcals	2592.20
Protein	g	88.11
Fat	g	49.17
Carbohydrate	g	479.23

Simple Shortcrust Pastry

Pastry helps to extend a meal by making pies or flans. Recipe books often make a great mystery of making pastry but it is not very difficult. Wholemeal flour makes a heavier, but more flavoursome pastry. If your family finds it hard to get used to, try using half wholemeal flour and half white flour. This will make a pastry closer to the texture they are used to. You have probably been told it is essential to keep everything cold but wholemeal pastry is easier to handle if the ingredients are cold when mixing, and the dough at room temperature for rolling.

Uses for shortcrust pastry:
As a flan base for vegetable quiche (p57), spiced lentil flan (p84); as a pie topping for Grandad's meat and potato pie (p103); over any lightly stewed fruit as a pudding; to line bun tins for jam tarts which can be made with homemade jam or stewed fruit; mince pies.

Nutrient	Units	per case
Energy	Kcals	1773.75
Protein	g	24.12
Fat	g	105.37
Carbohydrate	g	194.25

Quantities for a flan case, or large pie top:

250 g	flour	8 oz
125 g	fat (see below)	4 oz
	cold water	

A note about ingredients: Use white or wholemeal flour, or a combination of both. Up to a quarter of the quantity could be soya flour, thereby enriching the pastry with extra protein. Half plain and half self-raising will give a very short crumbly texture. The fat can be butter or margarine, and half lard or other hard white cooking fat.

Rub the fat into the flour with finger tips until, in the traditional recipe book phrase, the mixture looks like breadcrumbs. At this stage the crumb mixture can be frozen, and used as needed for pastry or crumble toppings without thawing first. Add cold water very gradually, blending it in with a knife. Stop adding water just before you think it's enough. The mixture will still be quite dry and crumbly. Use one hand to bring the dough together. If it is too dry and won't stick, a very little, just a few drops at a time, extra water will be needed. If it gets too wet, carefully add more flour. Turn the dough onto a floured board, and roll and use as required. Provided you don't overwork the dough, you will get good results.

Basic Sweet Pastry

This is a rich shortcrust suitable for sweet flans and pies. It is more sticky than ordinary shortcrust so it needs to be chilled before it's rolled out.

150 g	flour (wholewheat or white, or mixed)	6 oz
75 g	butter or margarine	3 oz
25 g	caster sugar	1 oz
1	egg yolk	1
1 tbsp	cold water	1 tbsp

Nutrient	Units	per recipe
Energy	Kcals	829.75
Protein	g	34.00
Fat	g	26.53
Carbohydrate	g	121.13

Rub the butter or margarine into the flour with your fingers until the mixture resembles fine breadcrumbs. Add the sugar and mix evenly. Beat the egg yolk with the water in a small bowl and then pour into the flour mixture. Mix together to form a firm dough. Turn the dough out onto a lightly floured surface and knead until it is smooth. Cover the dough and chill for about 30 minutes. Roll out and use as for basic shortcrust.

Cheese and Marmite Snacks

V Q Ch

Toddlers and young children like playing with dough, and with a little help, could make these themselves.

shortcrust pastry trimmings
yeast extract such as Marmite
grated cheese
milk
Parmesan cheese and sesame seeds

Roll out the pastry on a floured board. Spread half with yeast extract, sprinkle with grated cheese, and fold over the remaining pastry. Brush with milk, sprinkle with Parmesan and sesame seeds. Cut the pastry into narrow fingers and bake in a moderate oven for about 10 minutes, until lightly browned.

Basic Batter Mix

This basic batter mix is very versatile, it's a wonderful and popular way of giving children milk and eggs without them realising it !

125 g	plain flour	4 oz
1	egg	1
	milk	

Sieve the flour into a bowl. Add the egg and mix in. Add milk very gradually, beating well after each addition to avoid lumps. The final consistency should be like that of cream. (If there are still lumps, pass the mixture through a sieve.) There will be about 500 ml (nearly one pint).

Uses

Yorkshire puddings: Put a drop of oil in each cup of a twelve cup bun tin. Place the tin in a hot oven for a few minutes to let the oil get really hot. Pour batter into each cup, and return to oven. The puddings will puff up and brown in about twenty minutes. Remove from oven and serve immediately. Provided the tin was very hot before the batter was added, the puddings should not stick. These are a useful alternative to potatoes with any meal.

Nutrient	Units	per portn
Energy	Kcals	829.75
Protein	g	34.00
Fat	g	26.53
Carbohydrate	g	121.13

Variations: It is important to use plain flour. Otherwise you can use white and wholemeal flour in whatever quantities you prefer. Wholemeal flour will make the pancakes heavier and is more suited to savoury recipes. You can replace up to half the flour with soya flour, or fine oatmeal. You can replace up to half the milk with water or use soya milk. The quantities given will serve two adults. If you have a hungry hoard to feed, expect to double or even triple the amount of flour, and milk. The extra eggs are desirable, indeed any spare egg yolks you might have can be added to a batter mixture. However, if you want to make a triple quantity, and only have two eggs, they will do for up to 375 g (12 oz) of flour.

Pancakes: Preheat a heavy frying pan, and brush with oil. Make sure the pan is nearly smoking hot, pour in one to two ladles of batter, swirl around pan to spread it evenly over the pan base. Once the pan is really hot for the first pancake, turn the heat down to keep the pan hot but not smoking. When the mixture is set on top, use a spatula to turn the pancake, and brown the other side. (You can try tossing them if you like, and give the family some fun, especially if it is Shrove Tuesday.) Serve in the traditional way with lemon or orange juice and sugar or honey, for a treat. Or fill with a savoury sauce, top with cheese and bake in the oven to brown for a substantial meal. Any sauce you would use to layer lasagne works equally well with pancakes. You could try bolognese sauce (p101); tomato sauce with lightly cooked mushroom, courgette and peppers; tomato sauce with lightly cooked celery and fennel; mushrooms with bacon and sweetcorn; smoked fish in tomato or white sauce. See also the suggestions for uses of white sauce on p46. For children, make small pancakes, two or three at a time, sprinkle with cheese and a few sesame seeds, and brown quickly under a hot grill. Also fritters are simple. To the basic batter add some sweetcorn or some prawns, then drop a spoonful of the mixture into the hot frying pan. When it sets, turn to brown the other side. Keep the fritters warm while cooking the rest.

Waffles: If you have an electric sandwich maker, you may have waffle plates. This batter mixture can be used, but should be slightly thicker, or you can separate the eggs, and whisk the whites before adding, to give a lighter version. Waffle irons can also be obtained for use on conventional cookers.

Toad in the Hole: Don't forget this traditional supper dish. Grill sausages (four to six for one quantity of batter). Pre-heat a baking tray with 2 tbs oil until the oil is very hot. Add the grilled sausages. Pour over the batter and bake in a hot oven until the batter has puffed up and is golden brown, about 35 minutes.

Drop scones (scotch pancakes) are an old fashioned tea-time treat. The method is basically the same as for pancakes. Use 225 g (8 oz) self-raising flour, plus 1/2 tsp bicarbonate of soda, to one egg. The batter should be thick, dropping, not pouring off the spoon. Drop one tablespoonful of the batter into the hot lightly greased frying pan for each scone. You can make three or four at a time. Turn them over when they begin to set and round the edges, and bubble on top. Keep warm in a clean cloth until all are ready. Best served warm with butter, honey or homemade jam.

Optional extras which can be added to the batter are: raisins, chopped herbs, or chopped and drained pineapple.

High Protein Fritters

V Q Ch

These are a savoury version of drop scones and ideal as a lunch or snack for toddlers.

25 g	oil or margarine	1 oz
100 g	(small carton) cottage cheese	4 oz
2	eggs	2
50 g	wholemeal flour	2 oz
1 tbsp	milk	1 tbsp

Beat together the oil or margarine and cottage cheese, beat in the eggs, then stir in the flour and milk. Drop tablespoons of the batter into a hot lightly greased frying pan, brown on both sides and serve warm.

Nutrient	Units	per recipe
Energy	Kcals	634.65
Protein	g	33.13
Fat	g	41.36
Carbohydrate	g	34.77

Soups and Sauces

Soups are usually placed with starters in recipe books. They are grouped with sauces here, because both usually need a good stock as a base.

Home made soups are a world away from the tinned variety. Freshly made with a stock, vegetables, pulses or grains, or meat, and served with bread, soup can be a satisfying, even rib-sticking meal in its own right. Good stock is the key. The more a stock is reduced - boiled down until there is half or less the amount of liquid you started with, the more concentrated the flavours. Here are three methods.

Basic Meat Stock

Variations: The bones from a lamb joint can be used in the same way and give the best stock for traditional lamb-based dishes such as scotch broth (p38).
A ham hock (ask your butcher) is cheap, and makes excellent stock for lentil or bean soups, at the same time providing pieces of cooked ham which can be served cold in a salad, or in a pie.
Game carcases such as pheasant or rabbit give rich well flavoured stock especially good for mushroom soup (p41) or minestrone soup (p39).

This is one of the most economical uses for any left-over bones or carcases from a roast. Why throw them away when you can turn them into a tasty and useful stock?

1	cooked chicken carcase	1
1	large onion	1
1	carrot	1
1	bay leaf	1
	few black peppercorns	
	any other spare vegetables according to choice	

In a large pan, cover the cooked chicken carcase with water. If wished, add a cut onion, carrot, bay leaf, and a few black peppercorns and any other spare vegetables. Bring to boil and simmer steadily for as long as you like, at least one and a half hours. Strain, leave to cool and remove any fat that has settled on top. Season according to taste when using.

Basic Vegetable Stock

For vegetarians (or if you didn't have a chicken for yesterday's dinner). If you like, you can use the water that green vegetables have been cooked in. A pressure cooker will halve the cooking time. A dark vegetable stock can be made by frying the vegetables until browned, and adding soy sauce.

1	large onion	1
2	carrots	2
1-2	celery sticks	1-2
	bay leaf	
	thyme	
1.5 litres	water	3 pints

Chop the onion, carrots, one or two sticks of celery, gently fry in oil until soft, with herbs such as bay leaf and thyme if available, add the water, bring to boil and simmer for at least one and a half hours. Strain the stock, and discard the vegetables.

Basic Fish Stock

It is not all that difficult to slice open a whole fish and remove its innards, then clean it and cut off the head and tail, but if you really can't face it, a friendly fishmonger will do it for you. If you plan to make stock, ask to have the trimmings. Fish stock is easy to make and can be used in fish stew (p111) or to replace milk in a white sauce to which you are going to add fish.

	fish trimmings such as head, tail, fins or pieces of cheap white fish (but not the innards)	
1	onion	1
1	carrot	1
	few black peppercorns	

Simmer in water fish trimmings such as head, tail, fins (but NOT the innards), or pieces of a cheap white fish with onion, carrot and black peppercorns, for about an hour until you have a reduced and well flavoured stock. Strain, cool and use as required.

Never store ungutted fish. Clean it immediately you get it home and refrigerate it, well wrapped, and use within a day or two.

Making Soup

The following recipes all use the same basic method: lightly cook the onion until soft, add the other ingredients, and the stock, simmer until all ingredients are well cooked, liquidise if you want a smooth consistency, and taste for seasoning, which add to suit you own preference. (If a ham stock has been used it is very unlikely you will need any additional salt.) Regard the quantities given in these recipes as guidelines. The amount of stock you need depends on how fast or slow the soup is simmered, and for how long, whether or not you keep on a tight fitting lid, and how thick you like the end result.

If you don't have any stock, you can use water. It is just that a good stock definitely adds flavour and body. A very large stock pan (capacity at least four litres or seven pints) is recommended.

Leek and Carrot Soup

F V Ch

This quantity will give a thick and warming soup, served with wholemeal or cheese bread, for six people.

450 g	1 - 2 leeks	1 lb
450 g	3 - 4 carrots	1 lb
25 g	oil, butter or margarine	1 oz
750 ml	vegetable stock	1 ½ pts
1 tbsp	tomato purée	1 tbsp
	salt and pepper to taste	

Slice and fry leeks and carrots gently in oil for 5-8 minutes without browning. Add stock and bring to boil. Simmer until vegetables are cooked. Add tomato purée, liquidise and season to taste.
Serves 4.

Variation: Add about 25 g (1 oz) green lentils with the stock. More stock may be needed to prevent sticking.

GOOD SOURCE

Fibre	Vitamin B6
Vit A (ret eq)	Vitamin C
Thiamin	

Nutrient	Units	per portn
Energy	Kcals	134.49
Protein	g	3.11
Fat	g	7.44
Carbohydrate	g	14.55

Always drain and rinse tinned beans to remove the salt.

Butter Bean Soup

V Ch

Served with wholemeal bread, and sprinkled with chopped parsley or chives this is a very rich and filling soup with lots of protein.

2	large onions, sliced	2
3	sticks celery, chopped	3
2	carrots, sliced	2
1	large potato, cubed	1
25 g	oil, butter or margarine	1 oz
700 ml	vegetable stock	1 1/4 pts
300 ml	milk	1/4 pt
400 g	1 tin butter beans, drained	14 oz
	salt and pepper to taste	

Gently fry onions, celery, carrot and potato in oil without browning for 5-10 minutes. Add stock, milk and butter beans and simmer until vegetables are cooked. Liquidise and season to taste.

Serves 6 to 8.

GOOD SOURCE

Fibre	Thiamin
Vit A (ret eq)	Vitamin B6

Nutrient	Units	per portn
Energy	Kcals	125.72
Protein	g	4.58
Fat	g	4.86
Carbohydrate	g	16.97

Ham and Lentil Soup

F Ch

Use water or a vegetable stock, and this is suitable for vegetarians and vegans. Add tomato paste, or replace some of the stock with a tin of tomatoes for lentil and tomato soup.

1	large onion	1
2	carrots (or one carrot and one small turnip)	2
2 tbsp	oil	2 tbsp
175 g	split red lentils	6 oz
2 litres	ham stock	3 1/2 pts

Lentil soup seems to improve in consistency and flavour if left overnight in the fridge.

GOOD SOURCE

Vit A (ret eq)

Nutrient	Units	per portn
Energy	Kcals	90.76
Protein	g	6.75
Fat	g	0.49
Carbohydrate	g	15.84

Gently fry the vegetables in the oil until the onion is soft but not brown. Add the lentils and stock, bring to the boil and simmer for at least an hour. A few whole black peppercorns can be added with the lentils, but do not add salt if you are using ham stock. If you have used water, then salt can be added at the end, to your taste. You can liquidise the soup for a smoother consistency.

Serves 8.

Serving suggestions: with small pieces of cooked ham diced into the soup. Garnish with squares or triangles of toast and chopped parsley.

Scotch Broth

F Ch

This recipe is the real Scottish one. In the old days it would have had boiling mutton cooked in it, and the sliced meat served separately. It depends for its flavour on the combination of lamb and barley, and is always served with the pieces of vegetable whole. However, there is no reason why you should not liquidise the soup for a baby or young children who don't like 'bits' in soup.

50 g	dried peas or soup mix	2 oz
50 g	pot or pearl barley	2 oz
1	onion	1
1-2	carrots	1-2
1	small leek	1
1	small turnip	1
2 tbsp	oil, or dripping for authenticity	2 tbsp
2 litres	lamb stock or water	3½ pints
	seasoning to taste and chopped parsley to garnish	

Always drain off soaking water from peas and beans and use fresh water in which to cook them.
Salt dried beans and peas after they're cooked as salting toughens them.

Soak the dried peas or soup mix overnight. Chop all the vegetables into small dice, and gently fry in the oil until the onion is soft. Add the peas, barley and stock. Bring to the boil, boil hard for 10 minutes, then simmer until the peas are soft, at least one hour. Season to taste.

Serves 8.

Nutrient	Units	per portn
Energy	Kcals	86.51
Protein	g	3.52
Fat	g	3.25
Carbohydrate	g	11.54

Serving suggestion: with chopped parsley as a garnish and wholemeal rolls. Other vegetables can be added near the end of the cooking time, such as chopped celery, cabbage, broccoli, or fresh broad beans.

Variations: Rice can be substituted for the pasta, in which case add it with the main vegetables. 25 g (1 oz) of cooked haricot or black-eye beans can be added with the main vegetables.

Minestrone

F V Ch

Minestrone soup is traditionally served with the bits in, but can be liquidised for toddlers. The essential ingredients are the tomatoes, oil, garlic, pasta and the lightly cooked green vegetables.

A good variety of chopped and diced vegetables such as:		
1	clove garlic	1
1	small onion	1
1	carrot	1
1	turnip	1
1	leek	1
2	celery sticks	2
4	fresh tomatoes (or a 400 g (14 oz) tin)	4
1 tbsp	tomato purée	1 tbsp
2 tbsp	oil	2 tbsp
1.5 litres	stock	2½ pts
50 g	small pasta pieces	2 oz
125-175 g	green vegetables such as shredded cabbage, sliced green or runner beans, fresh peas	4-6 oz
	salt and pepper, to season	
	grated Parmesan cheese	

Gently fry the vegetables, other than the green vegetables, in the oil, until the onion is soft, then add the tomatoes, tomato purée, and stock. Bring to boil, and simmer for about 15 minutes. Add the pasta, simmer for another 10 minutes, add the green vegetables and simmer for a further 5-10 minutes, until they are just cooked. Season to taste.

Serves 6.

Serving suggestion: with crusty bread and grated Parmesan cheese to sprinkle over.

GOOD SOURCE

Vit A (ret eq)		Vitamin C

Nutrient	Units	per portn
Energy	Kcals	100.92
Protein	g	3.73
Fat	g	4.35
Carbohydrate	g	12.62

Watercress may be stored in the fridge in a plastic bag for up to five days.

Watercress Soup with Leeks and Orange

V Ch

Watercress is a valuable source of iron, calcium and vitamins. Washed, it can be served raw as a salad vegetable, and goes well with segments of orange. If you have only used half a bunch as a salad, the rest can be added to and cooked with a quantity of vegetable soup which is going to be blended, or a small amount added to tomato sauce for extra richness and colour.

1	small onion	1
1	small leek	1
2 tbsp	oil	2 tbsp
1	bunch watercress	1
1 dsp	green lentils	1 dsp
1 dsp	rice	1 dsp
1.5 litres	well flavoured stock	2½ pts
1	orange	1
	salt and freshly ground black pepper to season	
	plain yoghurt	

Chop the onion and leek and gently fry in the oil until soft. Roughly chop the watercress, including the stalks, and stir into the onions with the lentils and rice. Add the stock, and from half the orange, the grated rind and juice. Bring to the boil and simmer for about 45 minutes. Liquidise the soup, season to taste and reheat.

Serves 6.

Serving suggestion: swirl a spoonful of yoghurt through each bowlful, and garnish with grated orange rind or with a little piece of julienne orange peel. The yoghurt and orange really do lift the flavour of the soup, so don't be tempted to leave them out!

GOOD SOURCE

Vitamin C

Nutrient	Units	per portn
Energy	Kcals	71.87
Protein	g	2.79
Fat	g	4.08
Carbohydrate	g	6.42

There's no nead to peel mushrooms, you will lose the flavour. To clean them either rinse under the tap and blot dry with kitchen roll or wipe any grit off with a damp cloth or small brush.

Mushroom Soup

F V Ch

Don't expect something pale and creamy, as the one in tins. Homemade mushroom soup is real, dark, earthy and totally different. You could add slices of lightly cooked speciality mushrooms for interest. Several varieties are sometimes available in larger supermarkets.

1	onion	1
250 g	mushrooms	8 oz
25 g	green or brown lentils	1 oz
1 tbsp	tomato paste	1
2 tbsp	oil	2 tbsp
1 litre	well flavoured stock	1 3/4 pts
	salt and freshly ground pepper to season	
	chopped fresh or dried herbs	

Chop the onion and mushrooms, and fry them in the oil until the onions are starting to turn brown. Stir in the tomato purée and lentils, add the stock and some chopped fresh or dried herbs such as thyme, tarragon, marjoram or chervil, bring to boil and simmer for about 45 minutes. Liquidise the soup, season to taste, and reheat.

Serves 4.

Serving suggestion: with a swirl of cream or yoghurt, a garnish of whatever herbs you have used, and wholemeal rolls to accompany.

Nutrient	Units	per portn
Energy	Kcals	97.26
Protein	g	4.47
Fat	g	6.12
Carbohydrate	g	6.53

Fresh or frozen fish can be used to make this soup.

Fish Chowder

Q Ch

This fish soup is almost a meal in itself and can be made with any firm white fish such as cod, haddock or whiting.

250 g	white fish, filleted	8 oz
	bay leaf, thyme and parsley sprigs	
250 g	potatoes, peeled and diced	8 oz
1	medium leek, sliced	1
25 g	rice	1 oz
	pinch ground nutmeg	
300 ml	milk	½ pt
	salt and pepper to season	

Place the fish in a pan with 600 ml (1 pt) of water, the herbs either tied together or in a piece of muslin, salt and pepper. Bring to the boil, then simmer gently for 10 to 15 minutes or until the fish is tender.

Remove the fish from the pan with a slotted spoon, discard any skin and flake the flesh. Remove the herbs.

Place the potatoes in the cooking liquid with the sliced leek, rice and nutmeg. Cook, covered until the potatoes and rice are soft. Return fish to the pan, add the milk, and reheat. Adjust seasoning to taste if necessary and serve.

GOOD SOURCE

Thiamin   Vitamin B12
Vitamin B6

Nutrient	Units	per portn
Energy	Kcals	174.35
Protein	g	15.49
Fat	g	3.79
Carbohydrate	g	20.76

Tip: Browned flour can be kept in a jar and used for thickening soups and stews. Simply stir the flour in a dry pan over a gentle heat, or in a tin in a slow oven, until a rich brown colour.

Nutrient	Units	per/500ml
Energy	Kcals	331.60
Protein	g	3.07
Fat	g	25.42
Carbohydrate	g	24.16

Old Fashioned Brown Sauce

F V Q Ch

This recipe has been gleaned from my mother's post war book of recipes and household management. Now you know how they made gravy before the days of Gravy Granules ! It's additive and preservative free.

25 g	oil, margarine or dripping	1 oz
½	onion	½
25 g	plain flour	1 oz
500 ml	water or stock	1 pt
	seasoning to taste	

Slice onion thinly and fry until golden brown in very hot fat. Lift out onion. Add flour to fat and stir all the time over the heat until a rich brown colour. Gradually stir in the stock, add the onion and seasoning, boil for a few minutes. Strain if wished, and serve. This is suitable for vegetarians if oil, and vegetable stock or water are used.

Variations:
• Fresh tomatoes can be used, of course. For this quantity, use four or five fresh ones in place of the tinned tomatoes. Large beef tomatoes are particularly suitable for this. It is probably best to skin them. Cover them with boiling water for a couple of minutes, then remove them from the water and, handling carefully, it should be possible to peel away the skin from the tomato flesh using a fork and knife.
• For a richer version add other red vegetables, such as a grated carrot, a chopped red pepper, and 50-75 g (2-3 oz) red lentils. Add water, about 300 ml (3/4 pint). When cooking lentils, take care they don't stick to the base of the pan and burn. You may find that a child who won't eat meat will like this. The lentils provide protein. Double the quantities, and add cooked mince to half, making a more traditional Bolognese style sauce, for those who prefer it meaty.
• Add a dessertspoon of paprika, and a pinch of cayenne or chilli powder, and just before serving, stir in a spoonful of plain yoghurt for a goulash style sauce.
• Chopped fresh chives could be used to garnish.
• Add enough well-flavoured stock to make a soup. As with watercress soup, a garnish of yoghurt or cream and grated orange rind does something special for the flavour.

Nutrient	Units	per serving
Energy	Kcals	339.65
Protein	g	8.00
Fat	g	22.96
Carbohydrate	g	27.20

Red Tomato Sauce

F V Ch

This is the most basic tomato sauce which can be used on its own on Pizza, Pasta, or Rice or as the basis of other sauces and fillings for 6 pancakes (p30). It can also be added to soups and stews for extra richness.

2 tbsp	oil	2 tbsp
1	medium onion, chopped	1
1	clove garlic, crushed	1
1 tin	(400 g/14 oz) tomatoes	1 tin
1 tsp	mixed dried herbs, or fresh basil or oregano if available	1 tsp
2 tbsp	tomato purée	2 tbsp

Gently fry the onion and garlic until soft but not brown, add other ingredients, breaking up tomatoes, and simmer gently until most of liquid has gone. Liquidise if preferred, and season to taste. Cooking time is about 20 - 30 minutes. A pressure cooker is useful for larger quantities.

Tomato "Ketchup"

F V Q Ch

For a quick alternative to the commercial variety.

1 tbsp	tomato purée	1 tbsp
	orange juice	

Mix the tomato purée with enough orange juice to make desired consistency. This can be spiced up with a dash of any of the following, to suit individual tastes: lemon juice, vinegar, cayenne pepper, Worcester sauce.

Variations: Cheese sauce. Add 50-125 g (2-4 oz) grated well flavoured cheese. Try a dessertspoon of Parmesan in addition to Cheddar or Leicester.

Serving suggestions:

Cauliflower cheese - pour sauce over cooked cauliflower, sprinkle with grated cheese, sesame seeds and paprika, and brown under grill or in moderate oven.

Macaroni cheese: mix sauce with cooked macaroni and brown under grill or in moderate oven.

Mushroom sauce: add 50 g (2 oz) lightly cooked mushrooms, and 25 g (1 oz) Stilton cheese to make it special.

Serving suggestion: pour over jacket potatoes.

Leek sauce: Add a medium leek which has been washed, sliced and gently fried.

Serving suggestion: layer with lasagne, alternately with tomato sauce.

Combine variations: e.g. Mushroom Sauce with gently fried leek.

Serving suggestion: use as filling for savoury pancakes, but see next variation.

If you find a milky sauce too heavy, particularly with pancakes, substitute up to three - quarters of the milk with chicken or vegetable stock, or experiment with cottage cheese whisked into the sauce.

Serving suggestion: add cooked ham and chicken, place in a pie dish, cover with shortcrust or flaky pastry, bake in moderate oven 35 - 40 minutes, and serve with green vegetables.

A quick low fat, low calorie alternative for gently cooked mushrooms or leeks is to simply stir in three or four tablespoons of plain greek yoghurt over a low heat.

White Sauce

V Q Ch

This white sauce is the basis of many delicious sauces which can be used with pasta, to fill savoury pancakes or fill pies.

25 g	oil, butter or margarine	1 oz
1 tbsp	plain flour	1 tbsp
250 ml	milk (whole or skimmed)	½ pt
	seasoning to taste	

Warm oil or melt butter or margarine over gentle heat. Add flour and seasoning, and stir over the heat for 2 minutes, taking care that the flour does not burn. Add milk very gradually, stirring well after each addition to prevent lumps, until sauce reaches required consistency.

Nutrient	Units	per serving
Energy	Kcals	457.95
Protein	g	9.88
Fat	g	34.99
Carbohydrate	g	27.54

Vegetables, Salads and Dressings

WARM POTATO SALAD

POTATOES AND BITS

POTATO BAKE

POTATO CHEESE LAYER

ALTERNATIVE PIZZA BASE

POTATO SCONES

INTERESTING CARROTS

STIR FRIED RED CABBAGE

COURGETTE BAKE

VEGETABLE QUICHE

COUNTRY CASSEROLE

VEGETABLE PASTA SAUCE

COLESLAW

GRATED BEETROOT SALAD

CELERY SALAD

CHICK PEA SALAD

BROCCOLI AND FETA SALAD

MARVELLOUS MUSHROOMS

TAHINI DRESSING

HOMEMADE THOUSAND
ISLAND DRESSING

CHUNKY TOMATO SALASA

HOMEMADE HUMMUS

Fresh vegetables and salads provide lots of vitamins as well as contrasts in taste, texture and colour which give meals variety and appeal. They are essential in providing a balanced fresh diet. The magic thing about them is that they need very little cooking, and can often be eaten raw. Some of the vitamins they contain, for example, vitamin C, are easily destroyed in keeping and cooking, so the golden rule is eat it fresh and raw, or cook for as short a time as possible. Microwave cookery is said to preserve the goodness best, then steaming, then cooking in a minimal amount of boiling water. (Reserve the cooking water to make vegetable stock to add to soups and sauces.)

VEGETABLES

Our parents and grandparents used to boil vegetables to death with salt and bicarbonate of soda to preserve the colour.

Most vegetables are best simmered in as little water as possible for four to eight minutes until just cooked (perhaps a little longer if they are to be puréed for a baby). Test with a fork. Potatoes take about twenty minutes. It is possible to get used to the taste of unsalted vegetables (and find out what they really taste like). Put just a few drops of lemon juice in the cooking water, and a sprinkling of freshly ground sea salt and black pepper can be served at the table to individual tastes. Experiment with fresh herbs if available. Mint with potatoes and peas is traditional.

SALADS

You probably have a favourite range of salad vegetables that your family likes to eat. Grated carrot, apple or courgette are good for offering to toddlers. If you get bored with presenting the same salad mix, try presenting different combinations of just two vegetables.

For example

- grated carrot and thinly sliced green pepper, dressed in orange juice
- carrot chunks and apple chunks dressed with lemon juice
- cucumber and green pepper
- cucumber and grapes
- lettuce as a bed for cucumber or red and yellow peppers or green pepper and apple
- raw cauliflower florets with cooked red kidney beans, dressed with oil and vinegar or lemon juice to taste

Not to mention fresh tomatoes with herbs, peas fresh from the pod, or very lightly cooked green beans. Ring the changes for lettuce by using different varieties and other leaves such as cos, iceberg, endive, rocket, watercress. Plain yoghurt with chopped mint gives a fresh, sophisticated dressing for next to no trouble. Into any salad toss a dessertspoon of peanuts, cashew nuts, walnuts, sesame, sunflower, or pumpkin seeds to add crunch, flavour and protein, and raisins or chopped dates or apricots for interest, a touch of sweetness, and vitamins and minerals. However young children MUST be supervised when eating nuts, in case of choking and of course you should warn anyone you don't know well that the dish contains nuts in case they are allergic to them.

Your children might be persuaded to eat things they have grown themselves. Even if you don't have a garden, try growing mustard and cress, or bean sprouts on the kitchen windowsill. They can be eaten about one to two weeks after sowing, and are very nutritious. Lettuce, chives, and carrots can easily be grown in a trough or window box, and beans, peas and tomatoes in grow bags.

Vegetables to eat raw: varieties of lettuce leaf and greens: cos, Webb's, endive, chinese leaves, rocket; cabbage, white or red, finely sliced in coleslaw; tomatoes, sliced with basil or chives; cucumber, cut in sticks to dip in yoghurt; green and red pepper, sliced or diced; carrots, grated or in sticks; onions, including spanish onion sliced in rings, finely sliced leeks, spring onions; celery, sliced or in chunks or sticks with cream or cottage cheese; mushrooms, as they come or in a vinaigrette dressing; peas, straight from the pod.

Vegetables to simmer or steam until just cooked: green leafy vegetables including all varieties of cabbage, kale, spring greens, chinese leaves, spinach (needs no extra water); brussels sprouts; cauliflower, broccoli and leeks all of which can be served in a cheesey sauce; asparagus, regarded by many as a special luxury because of its short season; root vegetables, potatoes, carrots, parsnips, swedes, carrots, celeriac; celery; peas, runner beans, broad beans, mange-tout.

Vegetables to shallow fry in oil: onions; red cabbage (see recipe p.55); green and red pepper; mushrooms; courgettes; aubergine.

Vegetables to roast in the oven: (coat the vegetables with hot oil and place them in a moderate-to-hot oven): traditionally, potatoes, small onions whole or larger ones quartered, parsnips; green and red peppers, tomatoes.

Vegetables for young children: If your baby is capable of picking things up and putting them in his mouth, then there is no need to purée everything and spoon feed him. (See "How to tell if your baby is ready for solids" p.5). Carrots, potatoes, cauliflower, broccoli, green beans can all be cooked until soft and presented in small pieces. Grated raw carrot and courgette can be managed. Vegetable soups are ideal for dipping bread. Toddlers can crunch on raw sticks of cucumber, celery and red pepper or pieces of tomato with the skin off. Your child may not like everything, but is sure to like something! And don't forget that the vitamins and minerals in vegetables are also there in fruit.

The peel of a potato has lots of nutrients so don't peel any potatoes unless you have to. Skins come off more easily when potatoes are cooked.

Potatoes are cheap and filling. The good old traditional way with them is to have them boiled with every meal, or more often these days as chips. They are a handy first weaning food, either mashed, or in pieces or fingers for baby to pick up. Baked jacket potatoes with cheese or a mushroom sauce can make an easy lunch or supper. Here are some other ideas.

Warm Potato Salad

F V Ch

500 g	new potatoes	1 lb
1	onion	1
125 g	mushrooms	4 oz
1 tbsp	oil	1 tbsp
1	clove garlic	1

Boil new potatoes in their skins. Fry sliced onion and mushrooms in oil (with garlic if liked). When the potatoes are cooked, dice and mix with the onion mushroom mix, drizzle over a light salad dressing, garnish with either roasted sesame seeds or chopped chives and serve with green salad and cold meats.

Serves 4.

GOOD SOURCE

Vitamin B6   Vitamin C

Nutrient	Units	per portn
Energy	Kcals	128.31
Protein	g	3.15
Fat	g	3.35
Carbohydrate	g	22.82

Potatoes and Bits

V Ch

This recipe is ideal for using leftovers. It is important when saving food for later or next day to cool it quickly and keep it in the fridge. When reheating, the food should be piping hot. Frozen food which has been thawed should not be refrozen unless it has been cooked first.

enough potatoes for family, peeled, boiled and chopped up
And as many of the following as you like:
fried onion
cooked bacon
mushrooms
cooked peas
tuna fish
hard boiled egg
grated cheese

Put your choice of ingredients together in one flameproof dish and heat through in oven or under the grill. If it seems a little dry, a small amount of stock or tomato paste thinned down with water will moisten this dish.

Serving suggestion: can often be managed when you have "nothing in the house", in which case, you may not have much else to go with it! Again, a robust salad, made with cabbage, carrots etc, will give a fresh contrast in taste and texture. Freshly lightly cooked green vegetables such as broccoli would also go well.

You could add a couple of tablespoons of finely chopped fresh herbs to the mashed potato

Variations: Omit the cheese altogether, layer the uncooked potatoes with sauteed leeks and onions, and cover with a well flavoured stock. Bake until the stock is absorbed and the potatoes soft.

Potato Bake

V Ch

This is a sneaky way to introduce egg! A colourful salad goes well with this; it is also tasty with sausages or bacon. Some Parmesan cheese in the potato gives bite, and sprinkled on top makes a nice crust.

750 g	boiled or mashed potatoes	1½ lb
100-125 g	grated cheese	3-4 oz
1	egg	1
1	tomato, sliced	1

Add most of the grated cheese to the mashed potato and mix well. Add one beaten egg and seasoning to taste, mix well in, put in greased baking dish, sprinkle with grated cheese and decorate with tomato slices. Bake for 30 minutes in a moderate oven (190°C, 375°F, gas mark 5).

Serves 4.

Potato Cheese Layer

V Ch

Add a layer of sauteed leeks; try different cheeses.

750 g	potatoes	1½ lb
100-130 g	grated cheese	3-4 oz

Peel and slice potatoes and cook until just soft. Layer potatoes and cheese in a baking dish, finishing with a layer of cheese. Bake in oven 190°C, 375°F, gas mark 5 for 20-30 minutes.

Serves 3-4, and can be mashed for baby.

Serving suggestion: accompany with a sharp colourful salad.

Some topping suggestions
- sliced mushrooms
- blanched broccoli florets
- sliced courgettes
- grated cheese
- sliced black olives
- drained, tinned sweetcorn kernels

Nutrient	Units	per base
Energy	Kcals	893.50
Protein	g	14.09
Fat	g	42.39
Carbohydrate	g	121.41

Alternative Pizza Base

V Ch

A homemade pizza base that is quicker to prepare than a dough base and the children can help to decorate their own with their favourite toppings.

250 g	boiled potatoes	½ lb
50 g	butter or margarine	2 oz
110 g	self-raising flour	3-4 oz
	seasoning to taste	

Mash the boiled potatoes with the butter until smooth, sift in the flour and seasoning, and mix to a dough, knead on floured board until soft and elastic, then roll out to a 25 cm (10 inch) round and place on oiled baking sheet. Top with tomato sauce and toppings of your choice.

Serves 1 adult or 2 children.

Potato Scones

F V Q Ch

These are delicious at breakfast or tea-time. You can serve them with grilled bacon, sausages, eggs, mushrooms and tomatoes for a weekend treat.

250 g	boiled potatoes	½ lb
50 g	plain wholemeal flour	2 oz
	butter or margarine	

Mash the potatoes whilst still warm with melted butter or margarine and a pinch of salt. Work in the flour to make a dough. Roll out the dough thinly into a round, and cut the round in triangles. Prick the scones with a fork. Preheat a heavy frying pan or griddle and brush lightly with oil. Cook the scones just two minutes each side until brown.

Serves 4.

Serving suggestion: still hot, dripping with melted butter or margarine, or with grated cheese which has been sprinkled over and browned under the grill.

Nutrient	Units	per portn
Energy	Kcals	133.86
Protein	g	2.73
Fat	g	5.90
Carbohydrate	g	18.61

You lose a lot of flavour and nutrients when you peel carrots, so unless they are old or discoloured, it's best just to scrub them.

Interesting Carrots

F V Ch

This recipe has a hint of the Middle East, and could therefore go with a spicy bean pot and pitta bread.

500 g	carrots	1 lb
2-3 tbsp	oil, preferably olive	2-3 tbsp
3/4 tsp	ground cinnamon	3/4 tsp
1/4 tsp	cumin seeds	1/4 tsp
1	clove garlic	1
1	bay leaf	1
	fresh or dried thyme	
	salt and pepper to taste	
1 tsp	lemon juice	1 tsp

Peel and slice the carrots, and cook them until they are just done, eight to ten minutes. Drain the carrots, keeping about 100 ml (1/4 pint) of the cooking liquid. Keep the carrots warm. Finely chop or crush the garlic. In the pan, stir the oil, garlic, cinnamon, cumin, thyme and salt and pepper, over a gentle heat for about ten minutes, to blend the flavours. (This could be done while the carrots are cooking, if you don't mind having two pans to wash up!) Add bay leaf and the reserved cooking liquid from the carrots to the oil etc, simmer for another 10 minutes, then add the carrots to warm through. Remove the bay leaf, and serve with lemon juice sprinkled over.

Serves 4.

GOOD SOURCE

Vit A

Nutrient	Units	per portn
Energy	Kcals	96.34
Protein	g	0.91
Fat	g	5.94
Carbohydrate	g	10.36

Cabbage is a good source of fibre.

Stir Fried Red Cabbage

F V Q Ch

Cabbages, which are members of the cruciferous family of vegetables, are now thought by nutritionists to be especially good for you being rich in Vitamin C and having some Vitamin A.

¼	small red cabbage	¼
1-2 tbsp	oil	1-2 tbsp
¼ tsp	ground cumin	¼ tsp
	lemon juice	

Slice and chop the cabbage small, but quite coarsely. Discard the core. Heat the oil in a wok or large frying pan. Add the cumin and stir round for a minute or two. Add the cabbage and stir and cook until it is done to your liking, but not too soft. It is best with a bit of crunch, and should take only a few minutes to cook. Serve hot, sprinkled with lemon juice.

Serves 4.

Serving suggestion: with Special Baked Ham (p92).

GOOD SOURCE

Vitamin C

Nutrient	Units	per portn
Energy	Kcals	41.50
Protein	g	0.87
Fat	g	3.02
Carbohydrate	g	2.88

Breadcrumbs can be stored in the fridge in a sealed container for up to seven days. You can also use breadcrumbs to thicken soups.

Courgette Bake

V Ch

This is an excellent accompaniment to sausages, beefburgers, grilled meat, or on its own as a vegetarian meal with crusty French bread. Other vegetables can be added, such as red peppers, celery and aubergine.

6	courgettes	6
2	onions, finely sliced	2
2 tins	(400 g/14 oz) tomatoes	2 tins
1 tsp	dried basil	1 tsp
2	cloves garlic	2
1 tbsp	sunflower oil or margarine	1 tbsp
175 g	cheese	6 oz
75 g	fresh wholemeal breadcrumbs	3 oz

Cut the courgettes into slices about ½ inch thick, and dry on paper kitchen towel. In a heavy saucepan soften onion and garlic in oil. Add courgettes, reduce heat and cover pan. Cook until tender, stirring occasionally. Drain some of the tomato juice away from the tinned tomatoes, chop tomatoes and add basil. Mix grated cheese and breadcrumbs. Grease an ovenproof dish. Put half courgette mixture in the bottom, then half the tomato, followed by half the cheese/breadcrumb mixture. Repeat the layers. Put in preheated moderate oven for about 45 minutes until the top is nicely brown.

Serves 4-6.

GOOD SOURCE

Fibre	Folic acid (T)
Vit A (ret eq)	Vitamin C
Thiamin	Calcium
Vitamin B6	Magnesium
Vitamin B12	Iron

Nutrient	Units	per portn
Energy	Kcals	356.24
Protein	g	17.98
Fat	g	22.59
Carbohydrate	g	21.60

Gratin of Rice, Tomatoes and Courgettes (page 70)

Variations: the cheese can be omitted. Fry 2 - 4 rashers streaky bacon with the onion. For a larger flan case use 3 - 4 eggs and 175 ml (6 floz) of milk.

Vegetable Quiche

V Ch

You can ring the changes to this simple quiche by using other mixtures of vegetables, such as leeks or courgettes or whatever is in season.

Basic pastry recipe using 250 g (8 oz) flour etc (see p28-29)

1 tbsp	vegetable oil	1 tbsp
1	onion	1
1	small green or red pepper	1
25-50 g	mushrooms	1-2 oz
1	clove garlic	1
2	eggs	2
150 ml	milk	1/4 pt
1 tsp	dried milk powder	1 tsp
1 tbsp	natural yoghurt	1 tbsp
1/2 tsp	ground mace	1/2 tsp
	seasoning	
75 g	grated cheese	3 oz

Line a 18 cm (7") flan case with pastry. Peel and chop onions, slice and core the pepper, slice the mushrooms, crush garlic and fry all together gently in oil. Cool. Beat the eggs, milk, milk powder and yoghurt together and add the mace and seasoning to taste. Scatter most of the cheese, vegetable mixture and mushrooms in flan case, pour on the egg mixture. Scatter over rest of cheese. Bake in the centre of a moderately hot oven for 40 minutes.

Serves 4.

Serving suggestion: either with jacket potato, or warm crusty bread, and one of the grated salads (p60).

GOOD SOURCE

Vit A (ret eq)	Vitamin B12
Thiamin	Vitamin C
Vitamin B6	Calcium

Nutrient	Units	per portn
Energy	Kcals	625.60
Protein	g	16.10
Fat	g	39.89
Carbohydrate	g	53.97

Spiced Lentil Flan (page 84)

Trim and peel celeriac before using. If you have any left over from making this dish it is delicious grated as a salad mixed with some creamy dressing.

Country Casserole

F V Ch

You can change the taste of this casserole by using different vegetables according to the season but take care not to overcook them.

225 g	celeriac, cut into chunks	8 oz
175 g	swede, cut into chunks	6 oz
175 g	carrots, thick slices	6 oz
1	onion, diced	1
200 g	broad beans	7 oz
150 g	green beans	5 oz
300 ml	vegetable stock	1/2 pt
300 ml	apple juice	1/2 pt
1	bayleaf	1
2 tbsp	cornflour	2 tbsp
2 tbsp	chopped fresh parsley	2 tbsp
	salt and pepper	

Put all the vegetables, stock, apple juice and bayleaf into a pan, bring to the boil, cover and simmer for about 30 minutes, until the vegetables are just tender.

Blend the cornflour with a little cold water until smooth and stir into the pan with the vegetables to thicken the sauce. Cook for another 3-4 minutes. Season to taste and sprinkle with the chopped parsley.

Serves 4.

GOOD SOURCE

Fibre	Vitamin B6
Vit A (ret eq)	Folic acid (T)
Thiamin	Vitamin C

Nutrient	Units	per portn
Energy	Kcals	152.09
Protein	g	5.43
Fat	g	1.52
Carbohydrate	g	31.09

If fresh basil is in season you can use it instead of dried. Use about half a tablespoon of fresh.

Vegetable Pasta Sauce

V Q Ch

Pasta seems to be every family's favourite and a vegetable sauce on their pasta is a good way of introducing vegetables to children in managable quantities, if they're not very keen on them.

2 tbsp	oil	2 tbsp
1	onion	1
1	clove garlic	1
125 g	mushrooms	4 oz
1 tin	(400g/14oz) tomatoes	1 tin
1/2 tsp	dried basil	1/2 tsp
1/2 tsp	paprika	1/2 tsp
50 g	grated cheese	2 oz
1-2	beaten eggs	1-2
	optional extras - sliced courgettes, chopped green or red peppers, (chopped cooked bacon for non-vegetarians)	

GOOD SOURCE

Vitamin B12

Nutrient	Units	per portn
Energy	Kcals	153.50
Protein	g	6.88
Fat	g	11.53
Carbohydrate	g	6.00

Chop the onion, garlic and mushrooms, and fry them gently until soft, with any of the other optional ingredients. Add herbs, seasoning and tomatoes. Simmer and stir, breaking down the tomatoes, for about 10 minutes. Take off the heat and allow to cool. Mix together the cheese and beaten eggs, stir them into the tomato mixture over a very low heat. The idea is to heat the sauce through, cooking the added ingredients, letting it thicken, but without curdling the eggs. Therefore, keep the heat low, and keep stirring until you have a thick sauce.

Serves 4.

Serving suggestion: pour over spaghetti or any other cooked pasta.

You could substitute shredded celeriac for the shredded cabbage.

Coleslaw

V Q Ch

Use a 125 g (4 oz) cup or carton to measure:

1 cup	shredded cabbage	1 cup
1 cup	grated carrot	1 cup
1 cup	chopped or grated apple	1 cup
	equal quantities of: mayonnaise,yoghurt (plain)	
	lemon juice to taste	

A hand grater or sharp knife can be used, but for speed, use a food processor to prepare the salad ingredients. The amount of dressing required will depend on whether you like your salad smothered or lightly coated. A cup of mayonnaise and yoghurt combined should be more than enough.

Mix all ingredients in a bowl and eat soon after preparing.
Serves 4.

GOOD SOURCE

Vit A (ret eq)

Nutrient	Units	per portn
Energy	Kcals	149.62
Protein	g	1.69
Fat	g	12.16
Carbohydrate	g	8.86

If you buy fresh beetroot with the tops on or grow your own, don't discard the leaves, wash them and cook as you would spinach, or shred the leaves and use raw in a salad.

Grated Beetroot Salad

F V Q Ch

This salad is pictured on the back cover of the book; you can see how colourful and appetizing it is and even though it's crunchy, it's moist. It goes well with flans and quiches.

1	grated raw beetroot	1
2	grated raw dessert apples	2
2	grated raw carrots	2
	juice of a lemon or one tbsp cider vinegar	

Mix ingredients and dress with plenty of fresh lemon juice. Best made about one hour before eating.
Serves 4.

GOOD SOURCE

Vit A (ret eq)

Nutrient	Units	per portn
Energy	Kcals	38.60
Protein	g	0.59
Fat	g	0.22
Carbohydrate	g	9.20

Variations: the quantities of the ingredients can be adjusted to suit your own taste. Cubes of cheddar or edam cheese are fine, but a blue cheese such as stilton, or a variety of cheeses adds interest. Some dried fruit such as raisins or chopped apricot can also be added.

Celery Salad

V Q Ch

This is a variation on the theme of a traditional Waldorf salad. The original version created in the 1890's at New York's Waldorf Hotel only had celery, apple and mayonnaise; the chopped walnuts came later. Ours has cubes of cheese too. There's something in this salad for everyone to enjoy.

3	sticks celery	3
1	apple	1
50 g	walnut pieces	2 oz
50 g	cheese cut into small cubes	2 oz
	lemon juice	
	vinaigrette or yoghurt dressing	

Chop the celery and apple into small pieces, sprinkle with lemon juice, and mix with the walnut pieces, cubes of cheese, and dressing of your choice. Serve soon after preparing.
Serves 4.

Nutrient	Units	per portn
Energy	Kcals	184.23
Protein	g	5.24
Fat	g	16.72
Carbohydrate	g	3.45

If you don't have any red onions you could use spring onions in this salad.

Chick Pea Salad

F V Q Ch

Chick peas are high in protein, fibre and iron and they make a quick and easy salad if you use canned ones. You can mix any fresh herbs with them, such as basil or coriander, for an almost instant meal.

1 tin	(400g/14 oz) chick peas, drained	1 tin
1	small red onion, finely chopped	1
1	tomato, diced	1
6 tbsp	fresh parsley, chopped	6 tbsp
3 tbsp	olive oil	3 tbsp
1 tbsp	lemon juice	1 tbsp
	salt and pepper	

Combine all the ingredients in a bowl and leave to stand for at least 30 minutes to allow the flavours to develop.
Serves 4.

GOOD SOURCE

Vitamin C

Nutrient	Units	per portn
Energy	Kcals	159.96
Protein	g	5.44
Fat	g	10.43
Carbohydrate	g	11.87

Broccoli and Feta Salad

V Q

Broccoli is an excellent source of vitamin C and it is a vegetable that many children are happy to eat since they think the florets are like flowers.

500 g	broccoli	1 lb
1	red onion, thinly sliced	1
125 g	feta cheese, cubed	4 oz

Break the broccoli into florets and slice the main stalk into matchstick size strips. Either steam or boil for about 2-3 minutes. Then plunge broccoli into cold water, drain and dry. Toss broccoli in a bowl with the onion and feta and some vinaigrette or creamy dressing.
Serves 4.

GOOD SOURCE

Vit A (ret eq)	Vitamin C
Folic acid (T)	Calcium

Nutrient	Units	per portn
Energy	Kcals	169.81
Protein	g	10.65
Fat	g	12.18
Carbohydrate	g	4.50

Variation: Combine lightly cooked green beans with equal quantities of cooked red kidney and haricot beans, with a herby vinaigrette dressing, for a mixed bean salad. Add tuna fish to this and you have a substantial tuna salad.

Marvellous Mushrooms

F V Q Ch

There are as many versions of vinaigrette dressing as there are cooks and chefs. I have come to the conclusion that it is all a matter of personal preference, and whether or not you are coming to the end of your bottle of oil. Recommendations range from equal quantities oil and vinegar, to, usually, mostly (4/5) oil. Fashions come and go, as to which oils and vinegars to use. Balsamic vinegar seems to be all the rage at the time of writing. We are also told to use extra virgin olive oil. Both can be expensive. Ordinary wine or cider vinegar, and olive or sunflower oil are perfectly acceptable for everyday use. Why not be adventurous with what you have in the garden by using herbs to flavour oils and vinegars? Garlic, rosemary and tarragon work well. A few drops of sesame or walnut oil will give a different flavour. Whatever you decide to use, and whatever the quantities, this salad is simplicity itself.

250 g	sliced raw mushrooms	8 oz
	oil	
	wine vinegar	
	mustard powder	
	freshly ground pepper	
	herbs	

Just mix the dressing ingredients together in a blender or with a balloon whisk. It can be kept in the fridge in a screw top jar. Shake well before use. Toss the sliced raw mushrooms in the dressing and leave at least 10 minutes before serving. Delicious!

Serves 4.

Nutrient	Units	per portn
Energy	Kcals	50.91
Protein	g	1.15
Fat	g	5.01
Carbohydrate	g	0.35

Tahini Dressing

F V Q Ch

Tahini looks like smooth peanut butter but is creamier. It is of Middle Eastern origin and is made from toasted sesame seeds. Since it has a mild, delicate flavour this is very popular with children. This recipe can be used as a salad dressing or as a dip or spread served with pitta bread or raw vegetables.

4 tbsp	tahini	4 tbsp
2 tbsp	lemon juice	2 tbsp
2 tbsp	water	2 tbsp
1	small clove garlic, finely chopped	1
1 tbsp	chopped parsley	1 tbsp
	salt to taste	

Stir all the ingredients together in a small bowl.

Nutrient	Units	per portn
Energy	Kcals	373.62
Protein	g	11.81
Fat	g	35.49
Carbohydrate	g	1.94

To reduce the fat content of any salad dressing and to make a lighter dressing you can substitute a low-fat yoghurt for mayonnaise.

Homemade Thousand Island Dressing

V Q Ch

Creamy dressings moisten salads that may otherwise seem too dry but so many shop bought dressings have sugar and additives, making your own is healthier and so simple.

4 tbsp	natural yoghurt	4 tbsp
2 tbsp	mayonnaise	2 tbsp
1 tbsp	tomato ketchup	1 tbsp
2 tsp	fruit pickle	2 tsp
2 tbsp	chopped parsley	2 tbsp

Mix all the ingredients together in a small bowl.

Nutrient	Units	per portn
Energy	Kcals	278.48
Protein	g	4.38
Fat	g	23.46
Carbohydrate	g	13.28

Chunky Tomato Salsa

F V Q Ch

Since Mexican food is now popular with all age groups this simple salsa can be used as a dip with raw vegetables, toasted pitta bread or natural corn chips. It can also be used with grilled foods, such as homemade burgers or fresh fish or even an omelette.

5	large tomatoes, peeled, seeded and diced (or you can use tinned)	5
1	onion, finely chopped	1
1	fresh green chilli pepper, seeded and diced	1
2 tbsp	chopped coriander leaves	2 tbsp
2 tbsp	wine vinegar	2 tbsp
	salt to taste	

Combine all the ingredients and mix well.

Nutrient	Units	per portn
Energy	Kcals	134.47
Protein	g	5.63
Fat	g	1.89
Carbohydrate	g	25.55

Handy Homemade Hummus

F V Q Ch

Hummus is now available in tubs in most supermarkets but it is so quick to produce with a food processor that it's much cheaper to make your own with a few store cupboard ingredients. It is healthy and seems to go down well with children of all ages as a dip or sandwich filling with salad or in pitta bread.

1 tin	(400 g/14 oz) chick peas	1 tin
4 tbsp	tahini	4 tbsp
3 tbsp	lemon juice	3 tbsp
2 tbsp	olive oil	2 tbsp
2 tbsp	water	2 tbsp
2	cloves garlic, crushed	2
	salt to taste	

Place all the ingredients in the bowl of a food processor fitted with a steel blade. Process until smooth.

GOOD SOURCE

Magnesium

Nutrient	Units	per portn
Energy	Kcals	219.63
Protein	g	7.76
Fat	g	16.26
Carbohydrate	g	11.35

Rice, Grains, Beans, Lentils and Nuts

TOMATO RISOTTO

*YELLOW RICE WITH
BEANS OR LENTILS*

*GRATIN OF RICE,
TOMATOES AND COURGETTES*

FRUIT AND NUT PILAFF

AS-YOU-LIKE-IT RICE SALAD

TABBOULEH

*WHEAT BERRY AND
CARROT SALAD*

SPICED CHICK PEAS

*SWEET AND SOUR
RED KIDNEY BEANS*

CHICK PEA SUPREME

SOYA BEAN CASSEROLE

BEANS PROVENCALE

REFRIED BEAN DIP

RAINBOW BEAN SALAD

*LENTIL AND
BUCKWHEAT SLICE*

ONE POT BARLEY STEW

GREEK LENTEN FAMILY SUPPER

SPICED LENTIL FLAN

BRAZIL NUT ROAST

CHEESE AND NUT MOULD

RICE

Rice is a very useful filler which needs no preparation, just cooking. There are different varieties of rice, suitable for different purposes. Long-grain brown rice is nutritious and has a nutty flavour, and can be used for any of the recipes here. However round-grain brown rice is sometimes available from supermarkets and health food shops, and is better for risottos. Basmati rice is white with a delicate flavour and cooks beautifully using the method described below. Perhaps if your family needs to be persuaded to eat brown rice, mixing it with basmati will do the trick!

These recipes call for long-grain brown rice. This method for cooking rice is virtually foolproof. Take one cupful of rice, and gently stir in a tablespoon of oil over a low heat. Add two cups of boiling water (or stock). Cover tightly (use foil, if your pan lid is loose). Simmer over a very gentle heat until all the liquid is absorbed (about 30 minutes). Keep the lid on and the heat down, and don't be tempted to stir or check too often.

Cooked rice is an excellent early food for babies. It can be given moistened with some stock and mashed, for the baby to pick up with her fingers.

The following recipes can be served straight away, either on their own, or as an accompaniment to another dish. Rice dishes can also be served cold as a salad, or quickly reheated in some oil, an egg added omelette style, to give Egg Fried Rice.

Tomato Risotto

F V Ch

Experts say risottos should still be moist when served, so don't let the rice cook too dry.

1-2 tbsp	oil	1-2 tbsp
1	onion	1
175 g	brown or basmati rice	6 oz
1 tin	(400g/14oz) chopped tomatoes	1 tin
250 ml	vegetable stock	8-10 fl oz
	frozen peas or sweetcorn (optional)	

Chop onion and fry until soft. Add rice and stir fry for a minute. Add tomatoes and two thirds of the stock. Simmer until rice is soft, adding more stock if necessary. (A tight fitting lid and low heat

The proper rice to use for a true risotto is arborio rice but you need to stir the dish the whole time it's cooking, which is very time consuming, but gives that creamy quality with separate grains. You don't need to stir if you use brown or basmati rice.

GOOD SOURCE

Thiamin	Vitamin C
Niacin	Calcium
Vitamin B6	Magnesium

Nutrient	Units	per portn
Energy	Kcals	303.60
Protein	g	7.53
Fat	g	5.89
Carbohydrate	g	58.82

Variations:

• If this seems bland, season with salt, pepper, soy sauce perhaps a little curry paste, to taste.
• Raisins and allspice would give a Middle Eastern flavour.
• Other beans or chick peas can be substituted for the kidney beans.
• Substitute lightly cooked frozen mixed vegetables if in a hurry.

GOOD SOURCE

Fibre	Vitamin B6
Vit A (ret eq)	Vitamin C
Thiamin	Magnesium
Niacin	Iron

Nutrient	Units	per portn
Energy	Kcals	492.60
Protein	g	17.86
Fat	g	3.82
Carbohydrate	g	103.12

should help prevent sticking.) If using frozen vegetables, add them just before serving. Makes about three adult portions.

Serving suggestion: accompany with grated cheese.

Yellow Rice with Beans or Lentils

F V Ch

Combining rice with beans or lentils adds to the nutritional value of the dish, providing protein and vitamins.

350 g	brown long-grain rice	12 oz
1 tbsp	turmeric	1 tbsp
1	clove garlic, crushed	1
1	onion, chopped	1
1	carrot, chopped	1
1	stick celery, chopped	1
	red and green pepper, chopped	
1 tin	(420g/15oz) red kidney beans, drained or 100 g-200 g (4-6 oz) green lentils, according to taste	1 tin

If using lentils, bring to the boil, drain, pour on fresh water, and cook until soft but not mushy. Cook rice with turmeric (see method in introduction on page p 68). Gently fry other ingredients until cooked. Add to rice with red kidney beans and/or lentils. Heat through and serve.

Serves 4.

You could cook more rice than you need for this dish and freeze the rest in plastic bags or containers for up to 3 months.

Gratin of Rice, Tomatoes and Courgettes

V Ch

This could accompany a meat or fish dish or serve it with a big crunchy salad for a light family supper.

4 tbsp	olive oil	4 tbsp
1	medium onion, finely chopped	1
225 g	courgettes, sliced	8 oz
2	eggs	2
	freshly ground black pepper	
1 tsp	oregano	1 tsp
75 g	Parmesan cheese, grated	3 oz
4 tbsp	chopped parsley	4 tbsp
4 tbsp	cooked rice	4 tbsp
3 tbsp	fresh breadcrumbs	3 tbsp
4	large tomatoes, halved	4

Heat half the oil in a large frying pan and fry the onion gently for three minutes. Add the courgettes, cook 5 more minutes. Beat the eggs with pepper and oregano. Add the cheese, half the parsley and all the cooked rice. Stir onions and courgettes into egg mixture. Spread the rice egg mixture in a greased ovenproof shallow dish. Mix remaining parsley with breadcrumbs and more oregano and pepper to taste. Push halved tomatoes, cut sides uppermost into the rice mixture, easing them down until tops are level with the mixture. Sprinkle breadcrumb mix over entire dish. Drizzle remaining oil evenly over dish. Bake in pre-heated oven (190°C, 375°F, gas mark 5) for 15-20 minutes.

Serve hot.

Serves 4.

GOOD SOURCE

Vit A (ret eq)	Vitamin B12
Thiamin	Vitamin C
Vitamin B6	Calcium

Nutrient	Units	per portn
Energy	Kcals	362.03
Protein	g	15.63
Fat	g	21.35
Carbohydrate	g	28.64

Tip: Nuts have a high fat content, so shelled nuts can go rancid quickly - they can be stored in the fridge in an airtight container for 3-4 months or frozen for about 6 months.

Fruit and Nut Pilaff

F V Ch

This combination provides a delicious sweet savoury rice, similar to Middle Eastern dishes.

100-175 g	dried apricots or mixed dried fruit, soaked	3-6 oz
1	onion	1
1	green or red pepper	1
	oil for frying	
½ tsp	turmeric	½ tsp
¼ tsp	grated nutmeg	¼ tsp
	salt and ground pepper	
75 g	raisins	3 oz
350 g	brown rice	12 oz
1 litre	hot chicken or vegetable stock	1¾ pts
100 g	flaked almonds, toasted, or any nut mixture, chopped	3 oz

Soak the dried apricots at least two hours. Adjust quantity to taste. Peel and chop onion, core and deseed pepper, chop apricots. Heat oil, add onion and pepper and fry until soft. Stir in nutmeg, turmeric and seasoning. Add apricots and raisins, cook for a further 2 minutes. Add rice and cook, stirring for another 5 minutes. Stir in the stock and bring to the boil. Cover and simmer for 20 minutes or until rice is tender and has absorbed all the stock. Stir in the almonds and serve hot.

Serves 4.

Serving suggestion: this will go well with a salad dressed with a yoghurt dressing, and a spicy curry.

GOOD SOURCE

Fibre	Vitamin C
Thiamin	Magnesium
Niacin	Iron
Vitamin B6	

Nutrient	Units	per portn
Energy	Kcals	613.40
Protein	g	14.33
Fat	g	19.91
Carbohydrate	g	100.61

Variation: If you are using tuna in oil, omit the salad dressing. Simply mix in the tuna with its oil, and squeeze over about a tablespoon of lemon juice.

As-you-like-it Rice Salad

F V Q Ch

You can vary the quantities of the ingredients to suit the number of people there are to feed, so it's ideal for a party or a barbecue.

	cooked rice	
1	clove garlic	1
1	small onion	1
125 g	mushrooms	4 oz
1-2 tbsp	oil	1-2 tbsp
½	green pepper	½
½	red pepper	½
	your choice of: fresh summer vegetables e.g. peas, broad beans, green beans, sweetcorn, cooked chick peas, nuts;	
	dried fruit such as raisins, sultanas, chopped apricot;	
	small tin tuna fish, or cooked chicken (for non-vegetarians)	
	your favourite salad dressing (see p64)	

Chop the garlic, onion and mushrooms and fry them in the oil until soft. If you wish, stir in some spices or curry paste. The green and red pepper can be cooked with the onion, or left raw. Cook any of your choice of summer vegetables which can't be eaten raw, but try to include some with a bit of crunch! Mix together the onions, vegetables, rice and fish or chicken with salad dressing, and fresh chopped herbs if available such as thyme, coriander or chervil.

Serving suggestion: an ideal dish to bring to a Pot-Luck Lunch where everyone contributes something.

OTHER GRAINS

If you investigate the shelves of your supermarket or health food shop you may find other grains to try. Most can be used in a similar way to rice. Couscous and bulgar wheat are very easy to prepare, all you do is add boiling water or stock and leave the grains to absorb the liquid. Bland in themselves, these grains make excellent bases for salads or stuffings. You might also like to try polenta, which sets and is then fried in cubes to accompany a tasty mediterranean-style or spicy vegetable sauce.

Tabbouleh

F V Q Ch

This delicious Mediterranean salad is quick, simple and nutritious. It's great in the summer for picnics and barbecues and is something any member of the family can help to prepare.

175 g	bulgar (cracked wheat)	6 oz
5 tbsp	olive oil	5 tbsp
5 tbsp	lemon juice	5 tbsp
1	bunch spring onions, finely chopped	1
50 g	fresh parsley, chopped	2 oz
4 tbsp	fresh mint, chopped	4 tbsp
2	tomatoes, finely diced	2
1	cucumber, seeded and chopped	1
	salt and pepper	

Soak bulgar in enough warm water to cover, for at least 30 minutes until all the water is absorbed. Toss with all the other ingredients, and salt and pepper to taste. The longer you can leave it to stand the more flavour it will have. Use it as a salad, as a sandwich filling or to fill warm pitta bread.

Serves 4.

Variations: Instead of the tomatoes and cucumber you could add 350 g (12 oz) of fresh or frozen peas (cooked if frozen or raw if fresh) to the bulgar along with the mint and parsley.

GOOD SOURCE

Vit A (ret eq)	Magnesium
Vitamin C	Iron
Thiamin	

Nutrient	Units	per portn
Energy	Kcals	306.51
Protein	g	6.29
Fat	g	15.03
Carbohydrate	g	37.55

Variations: You can add grated cheese to the mixture, or fresh green beans cut into small pieces or sliced celery. The combination of chewy wheat and crunchy vegetables is very refreshing.

Wheat Berry and Carrot Salad

V Ch

Packets of wheat berries (or whole-wheat grain) can be found in wholefood and health food shops. They can be mixed, when cooked, with a whole variety of vegetables to make nutritious, chewy salads.

225 g	wheat berries	8 oz
125 g	carrots	4 oz
3	spring onions (or ½ small red onion)	3
150 ml	mayonnaise	¼ pt
	salt and pepper to taste	

Cook the wheat berries in unsalted boiling water for about 30 minutes or until tender. The cooking time will depend on how fresh the wheat is. Drain and leave to cool. Grate the carrots and finely chop the onions. Mix the wheat, carrots, onions and mayonnaise in a bowl and season to taste. The flavour will improve if it is left to stand a while.

Serves 6.

GOOD SOURCE

Vit A (ret eq)

Nutrient	Units	per portn
Energy	Kcals	297.21
Protein	g	5.24
Fat	g	19.81
Carbohydrate	g	26.15

BEANS, LENTILS AND NUTS

Beans are another inexpensive source of protein, vitamins and fibre. Pre-soaking and changing the water before cooking are said to help reduce problems of flatulence, but this isn't guaranteed! These recipes show that Beans don't mean Boring.

Beans must be thoroughly cooked. Generally they should be soaked overnight, then boiled hard for 10 - 20 minutes before simmering in fresh water for 1 - 2 hours, or even longer, depending on the bean. (A pressure cooker is a time saver.) They can also be Quick Soaked, which means bring to boil, boil for 2 minutes, leave to soak for at least one hour, then cook as above. All dried beans must be boiled hard for at least ten minutes at the beginning of the cooking time. Do not add salt to the cooking water, it toughens the skins.

A wide variety of beans is now available in tins, which saves the effort, and makes it possible to have a bean meal without preplanning !

Some cooking times for specific beans (after soaking):

	Open pan	Pressure cooker
Black-eye	1 hr	10-15 mins
Chick peas	1½ hrs	20 mins
Haricot	1 ½ hrs	15-20 mins
Red Kidney	1-1 ½ hrs	15 mins
Soya	3 ½-4 hrs	30-40 mins

Lentils do not need to be soaked and cook in twenty-five to forty-five minutes. (Split red lentils are quicker than green or brown lentils)

Spiced Chick Peas

F V Ch

If this version is not spicy enough, experiment with any other spices usually used in curries, e.g. coriander, cayenne, chilli, ginger, to suit your family's taste.

125 g	dried chick peas	4 oz
2 tbsp	wholemeal flour	2 tbsp
	choice of spices e.g. cumin or garam masala	
2-3 tbsp	oil	2-3 tbsp

   Soak the chick peas overnight, drain, then cook in plenty of unsalted water 1 - 2 hours (or in pressure cooker 30 - 45 minutes). Drain the cooked chick peas and turn them into a bowl, sprinkle over the flour and spices. Black pepper and a little sea salt can be added to the cumin, or caraway seeds are another possibility. One or two teaspoons of spice will be enough. Put a frying pan over moderate heat with 2 - 3 tablespoons oil. Turn chick peas in the oil and fry gently, stirring until they are lightly browned. Serve warm or cold.

Serves 4.

   Serving suggestion: warm or cold as a side dish with a curry. Also a nutritious nibble instead of crisps.

Tip: ground spices quickly lose their flavour and wonderful aroma, so buy in small quantities and use them up quickly. Do not keep for more than six months.

Nutrient	Units	per portn
Energy	Kcals	185.13
Protein	g	8.15
Fat	g	7.63
Carbohydrate	g	22.31

Tip: If you've forgotten to soak
dried beans overnight you can
use a quick soak method. Put
beans in cold water, bring to the
boil. Remove from heat and
leave to stand for an hour. Then
cook in the usual way.

Sweet and Sour Red Kidney Beans

F V Q Ch

This is tasty and spicy and is even one to try with children who
think they don't like pulses or green peppers.

2	onions,chopped	2
2	cloves garlic	2
1-2	green peppers	1-2
1 tbsp	oil	1 tbsp
1 tsp	basil	1 tsp
1 tsp	oregano	1 tsp
½ tsp	chilli powder	½ tsp
1 tsp	cumin	1 tsp
500 g	red kidney beans, cooked	1 lb
1 tin	(400 g/14 oz) tomatoes	1 tin
	bay leaf	
1 tbsp	honey	1 tbsp
125 g	raisins	4 oz
1 dsp	wine vinegar	1 dsp

Saute vegetables, garlic and herbs in oil. Add the rest of the
ingredients and simmer for 25 minutes.
   Serving suggestion: with green salad and cooked brown rice or
pitta bread (see p25).
Serves 4.

GOOD SOURCE

Fibre	Vitamin C
Thiamin	Magnesium
Vitamin B6	Iron

Nutrient	Units	per portn
Energy	Kcals	305.28
Protein	g	13.71
Fat	g	4.16
Carbohydrate	g	57.02

Tip: If you want the celery in this dish to remain crunchy, just add to the pan for the last 10 minutes of cooking time.

Chick Pea Supreme

V Ch

You can use any vegetable in season in this versatile dish but the celery does give a distinctive flavour.

125 g	dried chickpeas, soaked overnight then boiled until soft	4 oz
1	onion, chopped	1
1	green pepper, chopped	1
2	sticks celery, chopped	2
3	carrots, chopped or sliced	3
2 tbsp	oil	2 tbsp
2 tbsp	flour	2 tbsp
250 ml	milk	½ pt
	mixed herbs and seasoning	

Saute chopped vegetables in oil until fairly soft. Add flour and cook gently for 5 minutes. Pour in milk and stir until boiling and thick. Add chick peas, mixed herbs and seasoning. Simmer very gently for 15-20 minutes. Stir occasionally to prevent sticking. Add extra milk or water if sauce becomes too thick.

Serves 4.

Serving suggestion: with boiled rice. Can also be used as a topping over baked potatoes, or topped with breadcrumbs and butter and baked in the oven.

GOOD SOURCE

Fibre	Vitamin B6
Vit A (ret eq)	Vitamin C
Thiamin	Calcium

Nutrient	Units	per portn
Energy	Kcals	263.06
Protein	g	10.73
Fat	g	10.19
Carbohydrate	g	34.27

Tip: You can peel tomatoes by dropping them in boiling water for a few seconds, then using a slotted spoon transfer to a bowl of ice cold water, leave them for a couple of minutes and peel.

Soya Bean Casserole

V Ch

Soya is the only vegetable source of complete protein, which makes it particularly valuable to vegetarians, either in bean or flour form.

200 g	dried soya beans, soaked overnight and drained	7 oz
1	large onion, sliced	1
500 g	tomatoes,skinned and sliced (or1 tin (400 g/14 oz) tomatoes)	1 lb
1 tbsp	chopped parsley	1 tbsp
1 tbsp	chopped oregano	1 tbsp
	seasoning to taste	
250 ml	vegetable stock (or 250 ml (½ pt) water and 1 stock cube)	½ pt
25-50 g	low fat cheese, grated	1-2 oz

Cook soya beans in boiling water for about 3 hours and drain. Preheat oven at 190°C, 375°F, gas mark 5. Grease ovenproof dish. Saute onion for 3-4 minutes. Spread half soya beans in dish, cover with half onion, tomatoes and herbs, season. Repeat the layers, Pour over the stock. Sprinkle with cheese. Cover, bake for 30 minutes. Uncover and bake for 20 minutes until top is crisp and brown.

Serves 4.

   Serving suggestion: serve hot accompanied by crisp vegetable salad for contrasting texture.

GOOD SOURCE

Fibre	Vitamin C
Vit A (ret eq)	Calcium
Thiamin	Magnesium
Vitamin B6	Iron
Folic acid (T)	

Nutrient	Units	per portn
Energy	Kcals	241.43
Protein	g	21.47
Fat	g	10.80
Carbohydrate	g	15.65

Tip: In the summer if you have fresh herbs in the garden you can use these instead of the dried oregano; use combinations of whatever you have available, basil, thyme, rosemary.

Beans Provencale

F V Ch

Some chopped cooked streaky bacon and a teaspoon of black treacle will turn this into a quick version of Boston Baked Beans.

200 g	dried haricot beans,soaked overnight	7 oz
1 tin	(400g/14oz) tomatoes	1 tin
1	large onion, sliced	1
1	clove garlic, crushed	1
1 tsp	dried oregano	1 tsp
	salt and ground pepper	
1	small onion, sliced, to garnish	1

GOOD SOURCE

Fibre	Magnesium
Thiamin	Iron
Vitamin B6	

Nutrient	Units	per portn
Energy	Kcals	181.91
Protein	g	12.50
Fat	g	1.09
Carbohydrate	g	32.47

Cook the beans in boiling water for about 1 hour until tender, drain. Meanwhile break the tomatoes in a pan, and cook with onion, garlic, oregano and seasoning for 5 minutes to reduce liquid slightly. You may prefer to soften the onion in oil over a gentle heat first. Add cooked drained beans, and a tablespoon of tomato purée if wished, and simmer for 20 minutes.

Serves 4.

Serving suggestion: turn into heated serving dish, garnish with onion rings. A dash of soy sauce, added at the table, peps this up.

Tip: You could add some garlic or fresh chilli if you like for added flavour.

Refried Bean Dip

F V Q Ch

Here is a way of using a quantity of cooked beans. Traditionally made with pinto, black or pink beans, but any cooked beans can be used. If possible, cook the beans in a ham or vegetable stock. About fifteen minutes from the end of the cooking time add some fried onion. Drain the beans, reserving some of the cooking liquid. Mash the beans well. Heat 2-3 tbs oil over a low heat, and stir in the mashed beans, adding some of the cooking liquid to achieve the consistency of mashed potatoes.

Serving suggestion: in a bowl as a dip for tortilla chips, bread sticks or raw vegetables such as carrot, celery or peppers.

Variation: try a small handful of chopped coriander leaves mixed in with the beans.

Rainbow Bean Salad

F V Q Ch

This is a useful contribution to a Pot-Luck Party and the aim is to make it as colourful as possible.

¼ cup	(or 50 g) each of cooked and drained, or tinned	¼ cup
	red kidney beans	
	haricot beans	
	butter beans	
	green or runner beans	
	peas	
	sweetcorn	
2	spring onions	2
1	tomato	1
	vinaigrette dressing	
	green salad leaves	

Chop the spring onion and tomato, mix with all the beans, and the vinaigrette dressing, and serve on a bed of green salad leaves. It helps to mingle the flavours, if the beans are still warm when the dressing is added to them. Chopped fresh herbs of your choice will add interest. The quantities can be varied to suit what you have available.

Serves 4.

Nutrient	Units	per portn
Energy	Kcals	121.97
Protein	g	4.45
Fat	g	6.31
Carbohydrate	g	12.64

These slices freeze well.

Lentil and Buckwheat Slice

F V Ch

This makes a tasty picnic or lunch box snack.

1	onion	1
1	carrot, chopped	1
500 ml	water	1 pt
125 g	buckwheat	4 oz
150 g	red lentils	6 oz
2 tbsp	chopped parsley	2 tbsp
	salt and pepper to season if wished	

Saute onion and carrot for 10 minutes. Add buckwheat and remaining ingredients. Simmer for 15 - 20 minutes until buckwheat is cooked and water absorbed. Press into shallow dish. Bake at 200°C, 400 °F, gas mark 6 for 30 minutes. Serve hot or cold.

Serves 4.

Serving suggestions: try topping with grated cheese or sliced tomatoes before baking; use any leftovers to make sandwiches, with salad or chutney.

GOOD SOURCE

Vit A (ret eq)	Vitamin B6
Thiamin	Iron

Nutrient	Units	per portn
Energy	Kcals	279.45
Protein	g	14.15
Fat	g	1.25
Carbohydrate	g	56.46

Variations: For extra protein add cooked lentils or beans or cooked chopped meat 10 minutes before serving. Experiment with different vegetables. Serve roasted sunflower seeds or sesame seeds separately to sprinkle on top.

One Pot Barley Stew

F V Ch

This is easy to prepare in advance, and there's very little washing up. Extra herbs or spices can be added for extra flavour.

1	onion, chopped	1
2	carrots, sliced	2
1	small cauliflower, cut into florets	1
3	medium potatoes, diced	3
125 g	sliced mushrooms	4 oz
500 ml	vegetable stock	1 pt
2 tbsp	vegetable oil	2 tbsp
185 g	pearl barley (or pot barley available from health food shops)	6 oz
1	bayleaf	1
	ground black pepper	
1	teaspoon tamari or soy sauce	1

In a large pan, heat the oil and fry the onion until soft. Add remaining vegetables and barley. Stir well. Pour in stock and herbs. Leave overnight in fridge if possible. Simmer gently until stock is absorbed and the vegetables cooked (45 60 minutes). If preferred this can be baked in a slow oven.

Serves 4.

GOOD SOURCE

Vit A (ret eq)	Vitamin B6
Thiamin	Vitamin C

Nutrient	Units	per portn
Energy	Kcals	313.11
Protein	g	8.53
Fat	g	7.41
Carbohydrate	g	56.60

Tip: don't use red lentils for this dish, they don't hold their shape. Red lentils are ideal for soups or purées.

Greek Lenten Family Supper

F V Ch

Lent is a period of fasting in many faiths especially the Greek Orthodox. During Lent no animal products; meat, butter, cheese, milk or eggs, may be taken, so this Lenten dish of lentils and noodles is ideal for vegetarians and vegans alike.

250 g	green lentils, soaked overnight	9 oz
4 tbsp	(or 1 small tin) tomato purée	4 tbsp
1	medium onion, peeled and chopped fine	1
1	clove garlic, peeled and crushed	1
1 tsp	dried basil	1 tsp
4 tbsp	olive oil	4 tbsp
750 ml -1litre	water or vegetable stock	1 ¾-2 pts
250 g	noodles	8 oz
	salt and black pepper	

Into a large saucepan, put soaked, rinsed, lentils plus tomato purée, onion, garlic, basil, olive oil and water or stock. Bring slowly to the boil, then simmer for 30 minutes. Add the noodles and continue simmering for another 30 minutes, until lentils and noodles are soft. Additional water (or wine) may be needed to prevent drying out. Note that if "instant" noodles are used, the lentils should be cooked for 15 minutes before adding the noodles as the noodles will cook more quickly. Season to taste.

Serves 4.

Serving suggestion: a crunchy green salad gives contrasting texture.

GOOD SOURCE

Fibre	Folic acid (T)
Thiamin	Magnesium
Niacin	Iron
Vitamin B6	

Nutrient	Units	per portn
Energy	Kcals	551.12
Protein	g	23.74
Fat	g	16.18
Carbohydrate	g	82.90

This makes a good addition to a picnic.

Spiced Lentil Flan

V Ch

Silken tofu combined with lemon juice can be used for the topping instead of yoghurt. This is a useful alternative if anyone in your family needs a dairy-free diet or is vegan.

150 g	wholemeal pastry (made with 150 g/ 6 oz flour)	6 oz
150 g	split red lentils	6 oz
1	onion	1
1	clove garlic	1
1 tbs	oil	1 tbs
2 tsp	turmeric	2 tsp
1 tsp	paprika	1 tsp
½ tsp	ground cumin	½ tsp
275 ml	water	½ pt
2 tbsp	tomato purée	4 floz
	fresh or dried chopped basil	
2-3	courgettes	2-3
125 ml	(small carton) plain yoghurt	4 floz
	sesame seeds	

Finely chop the onion and garlic, and fry gently in the oil with the spices until the onion is soft. Add the lentils and water, bring to the boil and simmer about twenty minutes until the lentils are soft. It may be necessary to add a little extra water towards the end of the cooking time, but the consistency should be thick. When the lentils are cooked, beat in the tomato purée and basil. Add salt and pepper to season at this stage if you wish. Line a flan tin with the pastry. Wash and slice the courgettes and cook them lightly by frying or steaming for four minutes. Spread the lentil mixture into the flan pastry base, arrange the courgette slices on top, then pour over the yoghurt. Sprinkle with sesame seeds and bake in a moderate oven 30-40 minutes.

Serving suggestion: with fresh green crunchy salad.

Serves 4.

GOOD SOURCE

Fibre	Vitamin B6
Vit A (ret eq)	Magnesium
Thiamin	Iron

Nutrient	Units	per portn
Energy	Kcals	463.44
Protein	g	17.74
Fat	g	21.58
Carbohydrate	g	52.85

You could serve this with chunky tomato salsa (p65)

Brazil Nut Roast

V

This loaf can be served sliced hot with roast potatoes and vegetables, or cold with salad. It also makes a useful sandwich filler.

2	onions	2
1-2 tbsp	oil	1-2 tbsp
1 tsp	yeast extract	1 tsp
1 tsp	dried herbs	1 tsp
250 g	brazil nuts	8 oz
125 g	wholemeal bread	4 oz
1	egg, beaten	1
	salt and pepper for seasoning	

Finely chop the onions and fry in oil until turning brown. Add the yeast extract and herbs. In a food processor, using a metal blade, grind together the bread and nuts to make a uniform breadcrumb mixture. The onions can be included, or added to the bread and nut mixture afterwards. Bind all the ingredients together with beaten egg, and add salt and pepper to taste. Grease a 1lb loaf tin, spoon in the mixture and bake in a moderate oven for about 45 minutes until the loaf is brown on top and firm to touch. Leave the loaf in the tin for 5 minutes or so to cool, then turn it out.

Serves 4.

GOOD SOURCE

Fibre	Vitamin B6
Thiamin	Magnesium

Nutrient	Units	per portn
Energy	Kcals	562.70
Protein	g	14.55
Fat	g	47.71
Carbohydrate	g	20.07

Tip: If you don't have tomato juice, you could drain the juice from a can of plum tomatoes and use the tomatoes in another dish.

Cheese and Nut Mould

V Ch

This is a version of a nut roast which is moister than some with the addition of the cheese and tomato juice.

1	onion	1
1	clove garlic	1
2	sticks celery	2
2 tbsp	oil	2 tbsp
1 tbsp	wholemeal flour	1 tbsp
50 g	grated cheese	2 oz
175 ml	tomato juice	1/3 pt
125 g	wholemeal bread	4 oz
125 g	hazelnuts	4 oz
1 tbsp	oatflakes	1 tbsp
1 tbsp	chopped parsley	1 tbsp
1	egg	1
	salt and pepper to taste	

Finely chop the onion, garlic and celery. Fry them gently in oil until the onion is soft. Add the flour, cheese and tomato juice and stir until thickened. Grind the bread and nuts together in a food processor and mix into the tomato mixture with the oatflakes and parsley. Bind together with beaten egg and season to taste. Spoon into a 2lb loaf tin and bake in a moderate oven for about one hour.

Serves 4.

Serving suggestion: turn the loaf onto a serving dish and serve sliced hot with a tomato sauce (see p44) or cold with crunchy fresh salad.

GOOD SOURCE

Fibre	Vitamin B12
Thiamin	Calcium
Vitamin B6	Magnesium

Nutrient	Units	per portn
Energy	Kcals	439.17
Protein	g	14.01
Fat	g	32.31
Carbohydrate	g	24.77

Meat, Poultry and Fish

Meat, poultry and fish are an important source of protein, and red meat and liver also contain iron and the B group of vitamins. They are not cheap, and if you are concerned about how the animals are bred, raised and treated before slaughter, then seek out an organic butcher, but you will find organic meat more expensive still. The recipes in this section suggest some traditional and some economical ways of cooking and extending meat and fish dishes for all the family. A good butcher will gladly advise you on the best way to cook your choice of meat - cheaper cuts usually need long, slow, moist cooking.

ROASTING MEAT AND POULTRY

Roasting a chicken or suitable joint of beef, lamb or pork is very easy, and can be quite economical, as often a joint will give enough meat for a second meal, and a chicken will give a good soup or stock, too.

All you need to do is remove giblets if it is a chicken (they can be simmered separately for about 45 minutes to provide a gravy stock), place in a large covered tin or pyrex roasting dish, sprinkle with herbs and seasoning and cook in a moderate oven. The times usually given are twenty minutes per pound weight, plus twenty minutes. Pork should be well done, so allow twenty-five minutes per pound. A chicken can stay in the oven longer without coming to any harm, provided it is covered.

Serving suggestion: Once the joint or bird is in the oven you have at least an hour and a half to prepare the rest of the meal, or otherwise attend to your family's needs. Simply put some potatoes in the oven to bake in their jackets at the same time, then all you have to do is cook some vegetables or prepare a salad at the last minute.

Some quick and simple ways to enhance the flavour of chicken and its gravy juices:
- place a whole peeled onion inside the cavity of the bird
- put half a lemon or orange inside and grate the rind and squeeze the juice from the other half over the top
- smother the bird with chopped fresh or dried herbs such as thyme, marjoram, tarragon
- stuff the inside with a breadcrumb or rice stuffing (and include the weight of the stuffing when calculating the cooking time)

Top: Traditional Fish Pie (page 112) and
Bottom: Fish Cakes (page 118)

Variations: Herbs really do add taste and interest. Strongly flavoured ones work best, but beware of using too much. One or two teaspoons of fresh chopped sage, thyme, rosemary or tarragon should be enough. Other possible additions to the stuffing mixture are mushrooms, dried apricots or other fruit, hazel nuts or brazil nuts to replace the walnuts.

Easy two-in-one Walnut Suffing

F V

Use this stuffing to fill the cavity of a chicken or bake separately, to provide a Vegetarian Nut Roast.

1	small onion	1
1 tbsp	oil	1 tbsp
3	slices wholemeal bread	3
75 g	walnut pieces	3 oz
1 tsp	yeast extract	1 tsp
	hot water	
	salt and pepper to season	
	mixed fresh or dried herbs	

Chop the onion and fry it gently in the oil until soft. Break up the bread and place it in a food processor with the onion, walnuts and herbs. Use a metal blade in the food processor to grind all the ingredients to a uniform breadcrumb mixture. Dissolve the yeast extract in about half a cup of hot water. Turn the stuffing mixture into a bowl, add generous seasoning with salt and pepper, and gradually add just enough of the hot water and yeast extract to bind the mixture together.

To make a Vegetarian Nut Roast put the stuffing mixture in a loaf tin, and place the tin in a larger one containing about 1cm (½ inch) water. Bake in a moderate oven for about 45 minutes until the top is brown and the loaf feels firm. Serve sliced hot or cold, with seasonal vegetables or salad.

Double the quantities and you can stuff a chicken and make the loaf at the same time.

Nutrient	Units	per serving
Energy	Kcals	886.09
Protein	g	24.15
Fat	g	65.38
Carbohydrate	g	53.69

Spicy Lamb with Kidney Beans (page 94)

ROASTING MEAT AND POULTRY

As most of us are trying to reduce our intake of fat, I thought you may want to try the traditional Devonshire and, I think, Cornish way of roasting. The meat (beef, lamb, poultry etc) is placed in a roasting dish. In the case of poultry, the giblets, heart etc can also be placed in the dish. Roughly chop an onion and add to the dish, then pour in boiling water to a depth of 2-3 cm (1-20 inch). Place the dish in the centre or just below centre of the oven and cook for the usual length of time. More water can be added during cooking as necessary. The potatoes can either be added to the dish or baked in oil in a separate dish. The resulting cooking liquor can be used instead of gravy, or used to make a gravy. Or you can save it in the fridge or freezer, and after scraping off the fat (which will rise to the surface) use in soups, stews etc in place of stock, or try roasting potatoes in it, they are delicious.

Other Roasts

Lamb. Leg joints are leaner, shoulder usually cheaper. Roast as for chicken with lots of rosemary and onion quarters placed around the joint. A teaspoon of redcurrant jelly can be stirred into the gravy juices.

Pork. Again, leg is leaner, shoulder usually cheaper. Try roasting with sprigs of sage and pitted prunes placed around the joint, they come out succulent and sweet and complement the meat surprisingly well. Roast pork is traditionally served with Apple Sauce, which can be made simply by stewing a peeled and sliced cooking apple in a lidded pan on top of the cooker until it falls to a soft purée.

Pheasant. In season a brace of pheasant is good value for money. One bird gives enough meat for two adults, so for a family you will need a brace, and may wish to stuff the birds to extend the meal. Pheasant may sound like luxury, but is simplicity itself to cook. Roast the birds in a covered roasting tin with a lid, in exactly the same way as chicken. They weigh less, so will probably be ready in about an hour and a quarter. Serve with plain green and root vegetables or salad, and roast or baked potatoes. The meat is dark and full of flavour (it might also contain some shot, so check it carefully before serving to children), the gravy delicious, and the carcase makes the best stock ever for soup.

Turkey. Whole turkey is the traditional Christmas or Thanksgiving meal. Roasting it in the oven follows exactly the same principles as chicken. If you don't have a covered roasting tin big enough, then place it in an open tin, but cover the bird well with foil. Remember that a turkey weighs a lot more, and calculate the cooking time accordingly, at twenty-five minutes per pound plus twenty minutes.

Turkey can now be enjoyed all the year round. Butchers and supermarkets sell boned and rolled turkey breasts which are much more manageable for a family meal, and can be roasted, and served hot or cold. Look out also for turkey meat in steaks, diced or minced. It can be used as a substitute for beef in recipes.

Testing to see if your joint is done

Insert a skewer into the leg, or thickest part of the breast, if it is a chicken or other bird, or into the centre of the meat if it is another joint. The juices should run clear. A little pinkness in the meat of beef is often acceptable to those who like beef rare, and some people also like lamb this way. Pork and chicken and other birds must be thoroughly cooked, and should not show any signs of pink in the juices.

Tip: use a food processor to break up lumps in brown sugar but keep an eye on it or it will turn into icing sugar.

Special Baked Ham

F

A joint like this is good value because as well as making a hot meal it slices well when cold, and the very last leftovers can be used in a raised pie (see p156)

1.5 kg	gammon joint	at least 3 lb
	cloves (see method)	
1	carrot	1
1	onion	1
2	cloves garlic	2
1 dsp	dark muscovado sugar	1 dsp
1	can Guinness or similar dark ale	1

With a sharp knife score the layer of fat on the joint in a diamond pattern. Insert cloves into the crosses. Slice the onion and carrot and place in a roasting tin. Put the joint on top of the vegetables. Crush the garlic cloves and spread them over the joint. Sprinkle the dark muscovado sugar over it. Leave to stand for about thirty minutes. Open the can of Guinness. Pour one half into the bottom of the roasting tin and the other half into a glass. Cover the joint and bake in a moderate oven for twenty minutes per pound plus twenty minutes. Drink the remaining Guinness! (In the old days stout was recommended to breastfeeding mothers).

Serves 8.

Serving suggestion: sliced, hot, with stir fried red cabbage (see p55).

GOOD SOURCE

Thiamin	Vitamin B6
Niacin	

Nutrient	Units	per portn
Energy	Kcals	472.37
Protein	g	33.46
Fat	g	34.38
Carbohydrate	g	5.12

Uses for Cold Roast Meats

Any cold meats can be cut into bite-sized pieces and mixed with cooked rice or pasta and whatever salad vegetables are to hand, to give a cold rice or pasta salad; or sliced and served with mixed green, and tomato and herb salads, with baked potatoes; cooked chicken lends itself to quick chicken curry; cooked lamb combines well with red kidney beans in a spicy tomato sauce; cooked pork with vegetables for a chinese style sweet-and-sour stir-fry.

Chicken Curry

F Q Ch

More vegetables can be added with the onion such as carrot, celery and cauliflower. Also cooked lentils will make the meal more substantial. Other cooked meats can be substituted for the chicken, e.g lamb. Omit the meat altogether and substitute any cooked beans for a vegetarian version. Children sometimes surprise us by liking spicy foods!

1	onion, chopped	1
1-2	dessert apples, sliced	1-2
1-2 tbsp	oil	1-2 tbsp
250 g	leftover cooked chicken	8 oz
	curry powder or paste	
1 tbsp	wholemeal flour	1 tbsp
250 ml	water or stock	1/2 pt
25 g	raisins	1 oz

Curry paste can be bought in various strengths and styles and is a real improvement on powder, so worth the expense if you have a taste for spicy foods.

Fry onion and apple in oil for about 5 minutes. Add curry powder or paste, 1 tsp to 1 tbsp, depending on taste. Stir around then add up to 250 ml (1/2 pt) water or stock. Stir well, add raisins and simmer for 10 - 15 minutes. Add pieces of chicken about 5 minutes from the end to heat through.

Serves 4.

Serving suggestion: serve on a bed of cooked brown rice, and accompany with dessicated coconut.

GOOD SOURCE

Niacin

Nutrient	Units	per portn
Energy	Kcals	224.97
Protein	g	15.60
Fat	g	12.04
Carbohydrate	g	14.60

If you're using fresh lamb rather than leftovers, fry in the oil after the onion and garlic.

Spicy Lamb with Kidney Beans

F Ch

There are many types of curry paste now available, from "very mild" to "blow your socks off". How spicy you make the dish will depend on who is going to eat it. A teaspoon of the mildest curry paste will be enough to give a level of spiciness that is not over-powering, and children can cope with. Instead of curry paste, you could develop your own balance by combining garam masala, ground coriander, ground cumin, and chilli. This will be a matter of experimenting until you find what suits you.

1	onion	1
1	clove garlic	1
1-2 tbsp	oil	1-2 tbsp
1-2 tsp	curry paste	1-2 tsp
2 tsp	tomato purée	2 tsp
1 tin	(400 g/14 oz) tomatoes	1 tin
	well flavoured stock	
1 tin	(225 g/8 oz) red kidney beans	1 tin
125-175 g	small pieces cooked lamb	4-6 oz
25 g	raisins or sultanas	1 oz
1	lemon	1
	salt and pepper to season	
	fresh coriander (optional)	

Chop the onion and garlic and fry in the oil until beginning to brown. Stir in the curry paste and tomato purée. Add the tomatoes, about 100 ml (4 floz) of stock and the drained and rinsed kidney beans, and simmer for about 10 minutes. Transfer the ingredients to a casserole dish, add the pieces of lamb and the raisins, and the grated rind and juice of the lemon. Place in a moderate oven and braise for about one hour.

Serves 4.

Serving suggestion: with pitta or Nan bread, green salad and a yoghurt and mint dressing. Scatter a little chopped fresh coriander leaves over the dish before serving.

GOOD SOURCE

Vitamin B6	Vitamin C
Vitamin B12	

Nutrient	Units	per portn
Energy	Kcals	215.34
Protein	g	14.43
Fat	g	10.21
Carbohydrate	g	17.48

Variation: you can use other canned beans in this dish for a change of style and flavour, such as kidney beans or chick peas.

Pork and Bean Hot Pot

F

You can ring the changes with this recipe by adding one or two teaspoons of curry or chilli powder to the pan when frying the meat and onions. Make sure the powder cooks for a few minutes before adding the stock.

500 g	lean pork, cubed	1 lb
1	large onion, sliced	1
150 ml	stock	¼ pt
2 tsp	tomato purée	2 tsp
1 tin	(400 g/14 oz) of baked beans	1 tin
	salt and pepper	

Saute the pork in a little oil until browned and sealed. Add the onion and cook for a further minute or two. If adding curry or chilli stir in and cook too.

Add the stock and tomato purée and bring to the boil. Cover and simmer for 45 minutes. Stir in the baked beans and simmer gently for another 5 minutes. Serve with boiled or jacket potatoes or rice.

Serves 4.

GOOD SOURCE

Thiamin	Vitamin B6
Riboflavin	Vitamin B12
Niacin	

Nutrient	Units	per portn
Energy	Kcals	286.70
Protein	g	31.90
Fat	g	9.59
Carbohydrate	g	19.23

Variations: crushed clove of garlic, plus 1tsp grated ginger root and 1tsp chinese five spice powder can be added.

Stir Fry Vegetables with Pork

F Q Ch

If you choose to have fresh beansprouts rather than bamboo shoots, they need very little cooking, and can be added at the end with the meat.

2 tbsp	oil	2 tbsp
1	small onion	1
1/2	green pepper	1/2
1/2	red pepper	1/2
1/2	courgette	1/2
1	small carrot	1
50 g	mushrooms	2 oz
1 tin	bamboo shoots, or fresh beansprouts	1 tin
2	drained pineapple rings	2
300 ml	hot chicken stock	1/2 pt
1 tbsp	soya sauce	1 tbsp
1 tbsp	wine vinegar	1 tbsp
1 tbsp	tomato purée	1 tbsp
1 dsp	honey	1 dsp
125-175 g	small pieces cooked pork	4-6 oz
1 tbsp	cornflour	1 tbsp

Chop all the vegetables to equal-sized pieces. Using a wok or large frying pan, heat the oil, then fry the vegetables, adding them one at a time. Keep the vegetables moving in the pan, and the heat high, but cook for just about 3 minutes. Add the pineapple, stock, soya sauce, vinegar, tomato purée and honey, simmer for another 3 minutes, add the pieces of pork and continue simmering until the meat is heated through. If the sauce needs to be thickened, do it before adding the pork. Blend 1-2 tsp cornflour with a little cold water to make a paste, blend in some of the hot cooking liquid, then return it to the pan and mix well with the sauce. Simmer for at least 2 minutes, with the added meat.

Serves 4.

Serving suggestion: with rice or chinese egg noodles.

GOOD SOURCE

Vit A (ret eq)	Vitamin B12
Thiamin	Vitamin C
Vitamin B6	

Nutrient	Units	per portn
Energy	Kcals	231.06
Protein	g	12.38
Fat	g	13.38
Carbohydrate	g	16.30

You can buy chicken wings and use them to make stock by boiling with some aromatics, such as a bay leaf, some peppercorns, some chopped leek, spig of thyme and a stick of celery.

Grilled or Barbecued Chicken Wings

F Q Ch

Chicken wings, if you can find a butcher who sells them, are usually very cheap. They take very little time to cook under a grill or best of all, on a barbecue, and they are an ideal size for little hands, especially at parties, when they can be served warm or cold. This recipe is for a simple barbecue marinade but you can just coat them in a little olive oil.

	chicken wings	
	barbecue sauce:	
200 ml	tomato ketchup	8 floz
100 ml	vinegar	4 floz
3 tbsp	Worcester sauce	3 tbsp
2 tsp	mustard	2 tsp
	salt and pepper to taste	
	chilli powder or crushed garlic (optional)	

Mix all the sauce ingredients together. Prepare wings by cutting each in two at the 'elbow' and trimming off the frilly tip. Put wings in barbecue sauce to marinate for at least two hours or overnight in the fridge, in a covered dish. Grill or barbecue the wings for about 20 minutes, turning them once after 10 minutes and basting with the sauce.

BARBECUE SAUCE

Nutrient	Units	per serving
Energy	Kcals	277.70
Protein	g	8.19
Fat	g	2.87
Carbohydrate	g	58.42

BRAISED MEAT

Nowadays people seem to want meals that can be prepared all at once and in a great hurry. This meets the needs of working families where no-one is at home during the the day. But for the mother at home with babies and very young children, long slow cooking is sometimes a better option. You can prepare vegetables early in the day. Sometime mid-afternoon you spend a few minutes putting all your ingredients together, place them in the oven and more or less forget about them until you are ready to eat! The following are braised meat dishes which won't suffer for being left to cook away gently for longer than the recommended cooking time.

Variations: Try cider instead of stock. Or orange juice, and tarragon, and stir in half a carton of fromage frais or yoghurt at end of cooking time.

Braised Chicken Portions

Chicken portions can be placed in a covered pot with chopped sauteed onion, and stock, or tomato sauce, and other vegetables, such as leeks, mushrooms, celery. Bake in a moderate oven for 40 - 45 minutes. (Juices should run clear when the portion is pricked with a skewer.)
Serving suggestion: with boiled rice.

Mediterranean-style Lamb

F

An easy dish to prepare in advance and the marinade could be used on other cuts of lamb, such as a butterflied leg.

4	chump or loin lamb chops	4
2 tbsp	olive oil	2 tbsp
2 tbsp	red wine or wine vinegar	2 tbsp
1 dsp	tomato purée	1 dsp
1	clove garlic	1
1 tbsp	chopped fresh herbs such as chives, thyme, oregano	1 tbsp
1	onion	1
1 tbsp	oil	1 tbsp
200 ml	rich tomato sauce (p 44)	1/3 pt
100 ml	well flavoured stock	3 1/2 floz
50 g	cooked haricot beans (or use a small tin baked beans)	2 oz

GOOD SOURCE

Thiamin	Vitamin B12
Niacin	Vitamin C
Vitamin B6	

Nutrient	Units	per portn
Energy	Kcals	563.16
Protein	g	18.24
Fat	g	49.54
Carbohydrate	g	11.93

In a shallow dish which will hold the meat in a single layer, make a marinade by combining the olive oil, wine, tomato purée, crushed garlic and herbs. Coat the lamb in the marinade, grind salt and black pepper over and leave in the fridge for at least two hours, preferably overnight. Chop the onion and fry it until it is beginning to brown, add the tomato sauce, stock and beans. Tip the lamb, with its marinade, into a casserole dish, add the onion and bean sauce, season again with a little salt and black pepper. Bake in a moderate oven for 45-60 minutes.

Serves 4.

Serving suggestion: with Courgette Bake (p56) and new potatoes or crusty bread.

Variation: omit butter. Put all the ingredients in suitable dish and microwave, adding apricots at the end.

Lamb and Apricot Tagine

F

A luxury dish, for a special occasion.

50 g	oil, butter or margarine	2 oz
500 g	lamb cut into 5 cm (2 inch) pieces	1 lb
2	cloves garlic	2
½ tsp	turmeric or saffron	½ tsp
½ tsp	ground coriander	½ tsp
½ tsp	ground ginger	½ tsp
	black pepper and cayenne to taste	
	water	
2	medium onions, sliced	2
125-225 g	dried apricots, soaked overnight and chopped	4-8 oz
	juice of one lemon	

Heat oil or melt butter or margarine in a heavy saucepan, add lamb and stir until brown. Add garlic and spices. Cook for 5 minutes, add one onion and apricot soaking water (but not the apricots), lemon juice and enough water to cover the meat. Bring to boil, reduce heat, cover and simmer for one and a half hours, or until meat is tender. After 45 minutes add remaining onion. Add more water as needed, but sauce should be thick. When meat is tender add apricots and continue cooking until fruit is soft but not mushy.

Serves 4.

Serving suggestion: serve on a bed of rice with green vegetables, for up to six people.

GOOD SOURCE

Thiamin	Vitamin B6
Riboflavin	Vitamin B12
Niacin	Iron

Nutrient	Units	per portn
Energy	Kcals	402.38
Protein	g	28.61
Fat	g	23.92
Carbohydrate	g	19.59

The following recipes are for beef. At present the safety of beef is uppermost in people's minds and you may have decided against serving beef to your family for the time being. These recipes are included however in fairness to the contributors who offered and tested them, for those who are now happy about their source of beef, and for the time, which it is to be hoped will come soon, when we are all reassured that British beef is indeed safe to eat. Minced lamb, turkey, pork or venison can all be substituted for minced beef. Also, you can use a mincer or metal blade in a food processor to grind meat yourself. Meals made with minced meat are particularly good for toddlers who find it hard to chew food.

Bolognese-style Sauce

F Ch

This is very useful to cook in bulk and freeze. Use with spaghetti and Parmesan cheese, for Spaghetti Bolognese; or layered with Lasagne topped with a cheese sauce and baked in the oven until brown and bubbly; or topped with mashed potato and baked in the oven and heated through until brown on top, for Shepherd's Pie.

1	quantity tomato sauce (p44) (about 1 litre)	1
250 g	minced beef or other meat	½ lb
	salt, pepper, herbs to season	

In a large saucepan or frying pan, continuously stir and turn the mince over a gentle heat until all the pieces are brown and separated. If you want to, drain off the juices, which will contain fat from the meat. Mix the mince into the tomato sauce, add seasoning and herbs to your taste, and either simmer on top of the cooker, or in the oven for about 45 minutes.

Serves 4.

Really Easy Burgers

F Q

This is not a braised meal, but the burgers can be prepared in advance and kept in the fridge until you are ready to cook them.

Making your own burgers is very easy to do. For each burger you need 50 g (2 oz) of minced beef or other meat. Add salt and pepper. Shape with your hands to a round flat burger shape. Grill 4-5 minutes each side and serve in a roll with lettuce and fried onions if you like.

Variations: mix 1 tsp tomato purée and some finely chopped cooked onions to the beef mixture.
Minced lamb with herbs, or minced pork with a little sage and grated apple also work well.

GOOD SOURCE

Vitamin B6   Vitamin C
Vitamin B12

Nutrient	Units	per portn
Energy	Kcals	223.89
Protein	g	13.82
Fat	g	15.90
Carbohydrate	g	6.87

Nutrient	Units	per burger
Energy	Kcals	106.08
Protein	g	8.16
Fat	g	6.88
Carbohydrate	g	2.80

Minced Beef Stew and Dumplings

F

Lean minced beef usually contains less than 10% fat, whereas ordinary minced beef often contains twice that amount of fat, so it's better to use lean minced beef when you are not going to pour the fat from the pan after browning the meat.

1 tbsp	oil	1 tbsp
1	onion, chopped	1
750 g	lean minced beef	1½ lb
2	carrots, chopped	2
1	small swede, diced	1
2	potatoes, peeled and cubed	2
425 ml	beef stock	¾ pt
1 tin	(400g/14oz) baked beans	1 tin
	Dumplings	
50 g	suet	2 oz
125 g	self-raising flour	4 oz
	salt and pepper	

Heat oil and saute onion. Add minced beef and stir round to separate and brown. Add carrots, swede, potatoes and stock and cook for 45 minutes. Add baked beans. Make dumplings by mixing flour with suet and a pinch of salt. Add water to mix to a firm dough. Divide into four and place in stew. Cook for 20 minutes.

Serves 4-6.

Serving suggestion: with a robust green vegetable such as spring greens, and mashed potatoes or wholemeal bread to extend the meal.

GOOD SOURCE

Fibre	Niacin
Vit A (ret eq)	Vitamin B6
Thiamin	Vitamin B12
Riboflavin	Iron

Nutrient	Units	per portn
Energy	Kcals	415.32
Protein	g	32.49
Fat	g	15.80
Carbohydrate	g	37.96

Braised Beef

F

Braising steak can be cooked slowly in a moderate oven in a covered casserole dish, or on top of the cooker in a stew pan with a well fitting lid, with sliced or chopped onions (gently fried first), seasoning and enough water (or beer or cider) to cover, at least two hours, until very tender and falling apart. Other vegetables such as tomatoes, celery, leeks, carrots, and beans can be added. If potatoes are included, this is a meal in itself.

Grandad's Meat and Potato Pie

A great mid-week family favourite.

750 g	stewing meat	1½ lb
2	small or 1 large onion	2
750 g	potatoes	1½ lb
1	quantity shortcrust pastry (p28)	1

Braise the stewing meat and onions with water and seasoning, as in the braised beef recipe above. Boil the potatoes, cut into small pieces. Combine the cooked meat and potatoes in a large ovenproof dish, with enough of the meat cooking liquor, to moisten. Cover dish with shortcrust pastry, return to oven and bake until pastry has browned. Serve with plenty of whatever country garden vegetables are in season such as carrots, peas, broad beans, cabbage, sprouts. Use the rest of the meat juices to make a rich brown gravy.

Serves 6.

GOOD SOURCE

Thiamin	Vitamin B6
Niacin	Iron

Nutrient	Units	per portn
Energy	Kcals	416.10
Protein	g	31.48
Fat	g	14.91
Carbohydrate	g	41.57

Game is more readily available in supermarkets and general butchers than a few years ago. In season, it often compares in price favourably with the more expensive cuts of beef, lamb and pork. It is usually reared in a natural, non-intensive environment, and is lean and tastes very good. Pheasant has already been mentioned (p90). As well as being roasted it can be braised on a bed of vegetables as in this venison recipe.

Braised Venison

F

The venison will do very nicely if marinaded overnight in the oil and wine. The juniper berries give a very distinctive clean lemony scent and taste. Don't be tempted to leave them out.

1	small onion	1
1-2	small leeks	1-2
1	stick celery	1
1	carrot	1
2-3	tomatoes	2-3
2 tbsp	oil	2 tbsp
1 tbsp	tomato purée	1 tbsp
500 g	venison, cubed	1 lb
150 ml	red wine or well flavoured stock	¼ pt
8	juniper berries	8
	salt and pepper to season	

It's important to crush the juniper berries to release their flavour.

GOOD SOURCE

Vit A (ret eq)	Vitamin B6
Thiamin	Vitamin B12
Riboflavin	Vitamin C
Niacin	Iron

Nutrient	Units	per portn
Energy	Kcals	242.30
Protein	g	30.27
Fat	g	8.97
Carbohydrate	g	6.28

Chop the onion, leeks, celery, carrot and tomatoes, and fry in the oil over a medium heat until the onion is soft and beginning to brown. Stir in the tomato purée, then turn the vegetables into a casserole dish. Brown the cubed venison in the oil in the same pan, then tip out into the casserole dish, on top of the vegetables. Pour the wine or stock into the pan in which the meat was browned, and stir over heat, bringing to the boil, to loosen any residues in the pan. Pour the wine and residues over the meat, crush the juniper berries, add them with the salt and pepper to the casserole, cover and cook slowly in the oven until the meat is tender and falling apart, one and a half to two hours.

Serves 4.

Serving suggestion: with mashed potatoes and a selection of robust vegetables such as greens, swede, carrot, broccoli.

Rabbit Casserole

F Ch

Include some potatoes and other root vegetables, cut up into chunks, in the casserole, and you have a complete meal in a pot. 25-50 g (1-2 oz) lentils can be added, which will help thicken the juices, otherwise use browned flour near the end of the cooking time to make gravy (p43).

4	rabbit joints	4
2 tbsp	oil	2 tbsp
1	small onion	1
2	carrots	2
1	stick celery	1
300 ml	good stock	½ pt
1 tbsp	tomato purée	1 tbsp
	mixed fresh or dried herbs	
	salt and pepper to season	

GOOD SOURCE

Vit A (ret eq)	Vitamin B6
Niacin	Vitamin B12

Nutrient	Units	per portn
Energy	Kcals	222.37
Protein	g	27.33
Fat	g	10.48
Carbohydrate	g	4.85

Brown the rabbit joints in the oil, then place them in a casserole dish. Chop the vegetables, and fry them until the onion is soft and beginning to brown. Add the vegetables to the rabbit, stir in the stock, tomato purée, herbs and seasoning, and cook in a moderate oven for one and a half to two hours.

Serves 4.

Serving suggestion: with plenty of seasonal vegetables.

Variations: If your family is not too keen on liver, try reducing the amount of liver and adding more vegetables. Use other vegetables that your family likes such as green or red peppers, courgettes, bean sprouts. The sauce is delicious.

Liver Stir Fry

Q Ch

Liver is relatively cheap, but not always popular. Try this recipe, you might be pleasantly surprised.

2 tbsp	olive oil or other good cooking oil	2 tbsp
1	onion, sliced	1
1	leek, cut in half lengthways, then sliced thinly	1
1	large carrot, cut in thin strips	1
125-225 g	mushrooms, thinly sliced	4-8 oz
500 g	lamb's liver cut in thin strips	1 lb
1 tbsp	soy sauce	1 tbsp
1	small (125 g/4 oz) carton plain yoghurt	1

Heat oil over medium heat in large frying pan, or wok. Add the onion and leek and stir round for 2-3 minutes. Add carrots and mushrooms and stir for a further two minutes. Push vegetables to the side (or remove to another dish) and add the strips of liver. Stir them round until browned (about 4 - 5 minutes). Remove the pan from heat and add soy sauce and yoghurt, stirring down well into the juices. Return the vegetables to the pan, place it on a low heat, cover and simmer for a further 5 minutes.

Serves 4.

   Serving suggestion: serve with brown rice or wholewheat noodles or mashed potato, and green salad or peas.

GOOD SOURCE

Vit A (ret eq)	Vitamin B6
Thiamin	Vitamin B12
Riboflavin	Folic acid (T)
Niacin	Iron

Nutrient	Units	per portn
Energy	Kcals	324.93
Protein	g	28.73
Fat	g	19.06
Carbohydrate	g	10.30

George's Delicious Liver Casserole

F Ch

Add sausages, mushrooms or tomatoes and other vegetables such as carrot or celery. Some additional stock or water may be needed. The beauty of this dish is to combine whatever you have at hand.

500 g	liver, cut into bite-size pieces	1 lb
1 tin	(400g/14oz) tomato soup (or equivalent amount homemade tomato sauce)	1 tin
1	onion, chopped	1
1 tsp	mixed dried herbs or basil	1 tsp

Fry the chopped onion until turning brown. Place with the other ingredients in a casserole dish, cover and cook at 180°C, 350°F, gas mark 4 for at least one hour.

Serves 4.

Serving suggestion: with jacket or mashed potatoes and green vegetables.

GOOD SOURCE

Vit A (ret eq)	Vitamin B6
Thiamin	Vitamin B12
Riboflavin	Folic acid (T)
Niacin	Iron

Nutrient	Units	per portn
Energy	Kcals	298.97
Protein	g	26.47
Fat	g	16.41
Carbohydrate	g	12.04

Variation: Sliced mushrooms can be added, also whole black peppercorns and a dash of sherry or brandy for extra sophistication.

Chicken Liver Pâté

Ch

Chicken livers are quite inexpensive, available in frozen packs in large supermarkets, and very handy to keep in the freezer at home.

1-2 tbsp	oil	1-2 tbsp
1	small onion, chopped	1
1	clove garlic, crushed	1
250 g	chicken livers	8 oz
1-2 tbsp	tomato purée	1-2 tbsp
	herbs and seasoning to taste	
1	small (125g/4oz) carton cottage cheese	1

GOOD SOURCE

Vit A (ret eq)	Vitamin B6
Thiamin	Vitamin B12
Riboflavin	Folic acid (T)
Niacin	Iron

Nutrient	Units	per portn
Energy	Kcals	150.21
Protein	g	16.80
Fat	g	7.95
Carbohydrate	g	3.14

   Gently fry the onion and garlic until soft, rinse the chicken livers and add to the pan. Cook the livers and onion over a medium heat until the livers are no longer pink but still quite soft. Stir in tomato purée and herbs and seasoning. Put liver mixture in food processor, add the cottage cheese, and blend to a paste. Turn into a suitable terrine and refrigerate for at least six hours, but preferably overnight.

Serving suggestion: with toast or crusty bread and salad as a lunch or supper. This quantity goes a long way.

Serves 4.

Fresh Fish

The high street fishmonger seems to be an endangered species, but larger supermarkets often now have fresh fish counters with a very wide range. There may also be a mobile fish van who calls in your area, bringing fish direct to your door from the port, weekly, or less often in quantities you can freeze.

Fish is highly nutritious, particularly oily fish such as mackerel and sardines. Look out for cheaper white fish such as coley, and less common things such as shark, fresh tuna or swordfish which are surprisingly competitive in terms of price. (Grill them like steak.)

Any fresh fish such as cod, plaice, haddock, trout or mackerel is best cooked simply, either under the grill with a drizzle of oil or knob of butter and seasoning, or in the oven wrapped in foil. 10 - 15 minutes under a medium grill is often enough. Cooked too long and it becomes dry. Try sprinkling just a little Parmesan on white fish before grilling.

Naturally smoked haddock, cod and mackerel, without chemical dyes, are now more readily available. If you go on holiday to the North East coast of England, or the Scottish coast, you will very probably be within striking distance of a smokehouse where you can see fish being smoked the traditional way. Well worth a visit.

Fish is a particularly rich source of Omega-3 oils, which are especially good for a healthy heart.

GOOD SOURCE

Fibre	Vitamin B12
Thiamin	Magnesium
Niacin	Iron
Vitamin B6	

Nutrient	Units	per portn
Energy	Kcals	507.14
Protein	g	46.05
Fat	g	18.16
Carbohydrate	g	42.46

Fish in Foil

F Ch

The advantage of cooking fish in foil in the oven is that it takes a little longer (20-40 minutes, depending on its weight and thickness) but won't suffer as much if you are not quite ready when the fish is!

1	whole trout or mackerel per person	1
	oil	
1	small onion	1
50 g	medium oatmeal	2 oz
	salt, pepper and herbs to season	

Clean the fish and place on a large sheet of foil on a baking tray. Chop the onion very finely and fry it in oil until it is soft and turning brown. Add oatmeal, herbs and seasoning to make a stuffing mixture, stirring over the heat for five minutes. Spoon the stuffing inside each fish. Drizzle oil over the fish, wrap and seal it well in the foil, and bake 35-40 minutes in a moderate oven.

Serving suggestion: with new potatoes or chips, and peas.

You can use fresh or frozen fish for this dish, but make sure frozen fish has completely thawed first.

Mediterranean-style Fish Stew

F Q Ch

Fish is healthy - it's low in fat and calories and high in protein. It's perfect for busy families, it's the ultimate fast food.

1	onion	1
1	clove garlic	1
1 tbsp	oil	1 tbsp
2-4	tomatoes	2-4
3 tbsp	fish stock or water	3 tbsp
	lemon juice	
4	pieces white fish	4
	fresh or dried mixed herbs	
	salt and pepper for seasoning	
	parsley	

Finely chop the onion and crush the garlic, and soften them in oil over a gentle heat. Cut up the tomatoes into eighths, add them to the onion and cook for another 2-3 minutes. Add fish stock (p35) or water and lemon juice, the fish, herbs, seasoning and some chopped parsley if liked. Cover with a lid and simmer on top of the cooker for 15-20 minutes or in a casserole in a medium oven for 25-30 minutes.

Serves 4.

Serving suggestion: with boiled and sliced new potatoes or crusty wholemeal bread.

GOOD SOURCE

Vitamin B6	Vitamin B12

Nutrient	Units	per portn
Energy	Kcals	159.14
Protein	g	26.98
Fat	g	4.03
Carbohydrate	g	3.98

A few peeled prawns can be added to this fish pie.

Traditional Fish Pie

Ch

This dish can be prepared in advance and heated up from cold, in which case allow about 35 minutes, to ensure it is piping hot all the way through. It is nice to serve this in individual pots. A little ramekin dish can be used for a toddler's portion.

250 g	white fish of your choice	8 oz
300 ml	cheese sauce (see method)	3/4 pt
1 tbsp	chopped parsley	1 tbsp
	potatoes, in sufficient quantity for the numbers the meal is to feed	

Boil and mash enough potatoes for the family. Bake the fish in the oven with enough water to cover it, for 25-30 minutes. Once the fish is done, lift it from the cooking liquor, and flake it into a casserole dish. Make a white sauce following the recipe on p46, using the fish stock and making it up with milk to about 300 ml. Add 25 g (1 oz) grated cheese. Combine the fish with the cheese sauce in the casserole dish, and check and adjust seasoning. Spread the mashed potatoes over the fish and sauce. Bake in a moderate oven until heated through and brown on top, about 25 minutes.

Serves 4.

GOOD SOURCE

Thiamin	Vitamin B12
Vitamin B6	Calcium

Nutrient	Units	per portn
Energy	Kcals	303.49
Protein	g	18.78
Fat	g	13.61
Carbohydrate	g	28.15

A pinch of turmeric in the rice cooking water will make the rice yellow, which is attractive. A cheaper white fish can be used, but most often it is served with smoked haddock. For something special you could go to town with smoked salmon and prawns. Try adding a little grated lemon rind, and offer slices of lemon to squeeze the juice over.

GOOD SOURCE

Thiamin	Vitamin B12
Niacin	Magnesium
Vitamin B6	

Nutrient	Units	per portn
Energy	Kcals	409.42
Protein	g	17.11
Fat	g	16.69
Carbohydrate	g	50.81

Kedgeree

Ch

An old fashioned fish and rice dish that used to be served for breakfast. It makes a good light family lunch or supper dish.

250 g	long grain brown rice	8 oz
1 tbsp	oil	1 tbsp
500 ml	boiling water or fish stock	1 pt
50 g	butter	2 oz
1-2	hard-boiled eggs	1-2
2	fillets cooked or smoked fish of your choice	2
	salt and pepper to season	
	chopped parsley, optional	

Turn the rice in oil over a gentle heat. Add boiling water or stock and simmer slowly until all the water is absorbed and the rice cooked. Flake the butter into the rice, and stir it in. Flake in the fish, and chopped hard-boiled egg. Test and season to taste, adding chopped parsley if liked.

Serves 4.

Serving suggestions: real butter really does make a difference to this dish.

Fish and Vegetable Rice with Curry Sauce

Ch

There are two ways to adapt this dish for children. If your children don't like spicy foods, make the tomato sauce in advance without the curry. Reheat it in two batches, adding curry paste to one batch only. If your children are fussy eaters, it might be a good idea to serve the vegetable rice, flaked fish and chopped eggs in separate dishes at the table, so that people can choose which they will eat.

2	onions	2
2 tbsp	oil	2 tbsp
1	carrot	1
1	green or red pepper	1
125 g	mushrooms	4 oz
250 g	long grain brown rice	8 oz
500 ml	boiling water	1 pt
2	fillets smoked mackerel	2
2	hard-boiled eggs	2
2 tins	(400g/14oz) tomatoes	2 tins
2-4 tsp	curry paste	2-4 tsp

Finely chop one of the onions, and the carrot, pepper and mushrooms. Fry the onion in 1 tbsp of the oil over a gentle heat until it is soft and beginning to brown. Stir in the rice and other vegetables, add the boiling water, cover with a tightly fitting lid and simmer until all the water is absorbed and the rice cooked (about 30 minutes). Meanwhile, fry the other onion in the remaining oil, stir in the curry paste (the amount you use will depend on the strength of the paste, and how hot you like it), add the tomatoes, breaking them up with a spoon as you stir them in. Cook the sauce over a medium heat for about 10 minutes. Flake the mackerel into the cooked rice, add the chopped hard-boiled eggs, and serve with the curry sauce.

Serves 4.

GOOD SOURCE

Fibre	Vitamin B6
Vit A (ret eq)	Vitamin B12
Thiamin	Folic acid (T)
Riboflavin	Vitamin C
Niacin	Magnesium

Nutrient	Units	per portn
Energy	Kcals	562.57
Protein	g	20.62
Fat	g	26.59
Carbohydrate	g	64.37

Variation: smoked trout or smoked eel could be used instead of mackerel.

Smoked Mackerel Pasta

F Q Ch

Pasta is very popular with young children, because it is fun with its variety of shapes and colours and can be picked up with fingers, and is easy to eat. Some like it plain, perhaps with cheese grated over; others like it with chopped salad bits, especially fruity ones such as apple, grapes and raisins; and creamy, cheesey, or tomato sauces can all be used for variety.

500 g	dried pasta shells or spirals	1 lb
1	large fillet smoked mackerel	1
250 ml	thick red tomato sauce (p44)	½ pt
50 ml	orange juice	2 floz

Cook pasta according to instructions on packet. Meanwhile flake the mackerel into a large bowl, removing as many bones as possible. Warm together in a saucepan the tomato sauce and orange juice, reduce if necessary to a thick coating consistency. When the pasta is ready, drain it and toss in the bowl with the mackerel and tomato orange sauce.

Serves 4.

Serving suggestion: eat while still warm with crusty bread and a green leaf salad to accompany.

GOOD SOURCE

Fibre	Vitamin B12
Thiamin	Vitamin C
Riboflavin	Magnesium
Niacin	Iron
Vitamin B6	

Nutrient	Units	per portn
Energy	Kcals	701.41
Protein	g	26.51
Fat	g	23.45
Carbohydrate	g	102.620

Quick Mackerel Pâté

Q Ch

This is a great way to serve mackerel to toddlers.

1	fillet smoked mackerel	1
1	small (125g/4oz) carton cottage cheese	1

You could add a little chopped parsley, some fresh herbs or finely chopped chives.

Flake mackerel into bowl, taking care to remove all bones. Tip in the carton of cottage cheese, and mash together to form a paste. A blender can be used. Turn into a small terrine or pot and keep in fridge for at least a hour.

Serves 4.

Serving suggestion: on toast or homemade crusty bread.

GOOD SOURCE

Vitamin B6	Vitamin B12

Nutrient	Units	per portn
Energy	Kcals	163.38
Protein	g	11.40
Fat	g	12.81
Carbohydrate	g	0.66

Tip: If you want to fry the rissoles and ensure they hold together you could mix in a beaten egg to the potatoes and tuna mixture.

Tuna Rissoles

Q Ch

With salad, and granary bread, this makes an interesting lunchtime snack. The rissoles can be deep fried from frozen, or grilled.

1 kg	potatoes, boiled and mashed	2 lb
1 tin	(200g/7oz) tuna in brine or oil	1 tin
1	egg, beaten	1
175 g	crushed cornflakes	6 oz
	oil for deep frying	

   Mash together potatoes and tuna fish. When cool form into small rissoles. Coat in egg and then coat in crushed cornflakes. Drop into hot oil for 3-5 mins. Makes about 10-12 rissoles.

GOOD SOURCE

Thiamin	Vitamin B6
Riboflavin	Vitamin B12
Niacin	Folic acid (T)
Iron	

Nutrient	Units	per portn
Energy	Kcals	239.91
Protein	g	7.37
Fat	g	9.84
Carbohydrate	g	32.46

Smoer

F Q Ch

This is a South African dish which is served on a bed of rice, making it quick, economical and nutritious. This quantity will serve two adults and a small child.

1 tbsp	oil	1 tbsp
1	large onion	1
1 tin	(155g/5oz) pilchards in tomato sauce	1 tin
1 tin	(400g/14oz) tomatoes	1 tin
	a dash of tabasco sauce to taste	

   Fry onion, chopped, in saucepan, add pilchards and tomatoes, cutting up tomatoes. Add tabasco and simmer for 10 - 20 minutes to evaporate some of the liquid. Serve on rice.
Serves 4.

GOOD SOURCE

Vitamin B12

Nutrient	Units	per portn
Energy	Kcals	105.83
Protein	g	8.83
Fat	g	5.03
Carbohydrate	g	6.84

Variation: Tinned mackerel steaks in tomato sauce can also be used.

GOOD SOURCE

Fibre	Vitamin B12
Thiamin	Calcium
Riboflavin	Magnesium
Niacin	Iron
Vitamin B6	

Nutrient	Units	per portn
Energy	Kcals	421.79
Protein	g	25.61
Fat	g	19.73
Carbohydrate	g	37.74

Variation: Traditionally, fish cakes and similar, are coated in breadcrumbs before cooking. This is not absolutely essential if the mixture is firm, especially if you are grilling them. If you want to, however, here is how: have two dishes ready, one with beaten egg, the other with wholemeal breadcrumbs (which can be made with the metal blade of a food processor, a useful way of using slices which are somewhat dried out). Dip each fish cake, first in the egg, then in the breadcrumbs, to coat it. Then grill or fry on both side until heated through and brown on both sides.

Sardine Beananza

Ch

This is a popular supper dish for hungry children home from school.

1 tin	(400 g/14 oz) baked beans	1 tin
1 tin	(330 g/12 oz) sardines in tomato sauce	1 tin
500 g	potatoes, boiled and mashed	1 lb
25 g	melted butter	1 oz
50 g	grated cheese	2 oz

Place beans in ovenproof dish. Top with sardines. Cover with mashed potato, sprinkle top with grated cheese. Bake in a moderate to hot oven for 25 minutes.

Serving suggestion: with salad or green vegetables.

Serves 4.

Variation: Traditionally, fish cakes and similar, are coated in breadcrumbs before cooking. This is not absolutely essential if the mixture is firm, especially if you are grilling them. If you want to, however, here is how: have two dishes ready, one with beaten egg, the other with wholemeal breadcrumbs (which can be made with the metal blade of a food processor, a useful way of using slices which are somewhat dried out). Dip each fish cake, first in the egg, then in the breadcrumbs, to coat it. Then grill or fry on both sides until heated through and brown on both sides.

GOOD SOURCE

Niacin	Vitamin B12
Vitamin B6	

Nutrient	Units	per portn
Energy	Kcals	147.65
Protein	g	10.52
Fat	g	2.87
Carbohydrate	g	21.25

Fish Cakes

F Q Ch

These are a very useful quick lunch, especially if they have been prepared earlier. They freeze well.

Boiled and mashed potatoes, enough for your family		
1 small tin	(175 g/6 oz) tuna fish or equivalent any cooked or smoked fish	1 small tin

If using tinned fish, drain off the oil or brine. Mash together the fish and potatoes, seasoning with salt and pepper to your taste. Use your hands to shape into eight or ten rounds about 1 to 2 cm thick. Grill for 5-10 minutes until brown on each side.

Serves 4.

No and Low-Sugar Puddings

ICE CREAM SODA

MILK SHAKE

FRESH FRUIT SALAD

COMPOTE OF DRIED FRUIT IN APPLE JUICE

STEWED FRUIT CRUMBLE

FRUIT PIE

PIE FILLINGS

FRUIT FOOLS

FRUIT ICES

FRUIT JELLY

LOW-SUGAR QUICK-TO-PREPARE ICE CREAM

RICE PUDDING

BAKED SEMOLINA

JUNKET

IMPOSSIBLE PIE

Children are notorious for being "picky" eaters. So often it seems to be the "good for you" main meals and greens and vegetables they refuse to touch. Believe it or not, if you offer only a wide range of healthy foods, over a period of time your children are likely to choose a balanced diet that will meet their needs. There are many alternative sources of the most important nutrients. See Guidelines for a Balanced Healthy Diet (p11).

There are two schools of thought about puddings and snacks. One is that they are full of sugar, probably fat as well, and therefore to be discouraged, with the exception of fresh fruit. Another is to accept that children are very active, and growing, they need to refuel their energy tanks, and do get hungry between meals. Sometimes this can affect their moods and behaviour. (Don't you get ratty when you are hungry?) Mothers recognize late afternoon as a particularly difficult time. Toddlers still have small stomachs, and sometimes prefer to eat little and often.

So if your children are going to eat between meals, it is a good idea to make those snacks as nutritious as possible. Sticks of raw carrot, celery or apple, or bread or pastry fingers are easy to provide.

Sugar is the big worry for mothers. They know it gives a quick energy boost, is easily bought and eaten in the form of chocolates, sweets, and commercial cakes and biscuits, and it is often tempting to use these as a bribe for desirable behaviour. And fond relatives just love to "spoil" your little ones, don't they? The trouble is that sugar does children's teeth no good at all, and apart from carbohydrates, contains no other significant nutrients; and a taste for sugar-loaded foods tends to turn a child's preferences away from the healthy choices they could otherwise make.

Some mothers try to cut out sugar from their families' diets altogether. Others do their best to minimise the damage by visiting the greengrocer's rather than the sweet shop; providing puddings and snacks with a low added sugar content, using natural unrefined alternatives to white sugar where possible; and encouraging plenty of teeth brushing.

The following recipes are for the times when a pudding or dessert is needed - when you know your toddler just won't touch the main meal, or you are entertaining, or a snack will keep the hunger monster at bay.

Where sugar is in a recipe, if you use unrefined (Billingtons is a brand most easily available) you can tell yourself that at least there are some trace minerals still there - it is available in golden granulated, and light and dark muscovado forms. It adds flavour and colour as well.

Alternative sweeteners include honey, concentrated fruit juices, malt extract, and dried fruit, especially dates.

Bear in mind that unrefined sugars and alternative sweeteners such as honey and dried fruit, still contain sugars which stick to the teeth, so good dental care remains important.

Compote of Dried Fruit in Apple Juice (page 123)

The obvious healthy way to finish a meal is to serve a choice of fresh fruit. Apples, pears, bananas, oranges and grapes are usually available, and in season, kiwi fruit, peaches, nectarines, strawberries, raspberries, melons and pineapples. Most take very little preparation other than washing, and peeling. An apple or banana costs no more than a chocolate bar. If your children won't touch vegetables they can just as easily get their vitamins from fresh fruit. Soft fruit is an ideal first food for babies - try mashed banana, kiwi fruit, ripe pear, avocado, melon - and toddlers like pieces of apple they can hold. Grown-ups can be sophisticated and have a mature cheese and oatcakes or crackers with the fruit, and won't even notice they didn't have a "pudding".

But for when a pudding seems a must here are some ideas for what are traditionally called Nursery Puddings - they also tend to be very popular with partners who like to remember (or haven't quite grown out of) their own childhood. Most are easy and quick to prepare, but some need time to bake or set.

A note about the codes beneath the titles of these recipes: "Cheap" (Ch) puddings and cakes etc are those that cost under £1 for the ingredients at the time of testing. It is hard to find cake recipes that are entirely dairy free. Quite a few are egg and milk free, but contain butter or margarine. These are coded "E". You may wish to try using a vegetable margarine (read the labels carefully), or experiment by substituting sunflower oil.

Drinks

Young babies need nothing but breast milk. Full stop. (No gripe water, no extra boiled water in hot weather, just drink more yourself, no juice). During the second half of their first year, as they begin to eat other foods, they can be offered plain water in a cup with a spout. Later they can be offered diluted pure fruit juice. Toddlers and older children can have sugar free fizzy drinks by diluting fruit juice with sparkling mineral water. Healthy milk shakes are easy to make if you have a blender.

Ice Cream "Soda"

In a beaker or glass pour a small amount of concentrated apple and blackcurrant juice. Add a dessertspoon of ice cream (p127). Top with sparkling mineral water. Serve with straws and a longhandled teaspoon to scoop out the ice cream.

Not-Too-Naughty Chocolate Cake (page 142)

Variation: In the height of summer there is nothing to beat a combination of red fruits: strawberries, raspberries, redcurrants, cherries, with nectarine slices.

Milk Shake

3/4	beaker milk	3/4
1	banana	1
1 dsp	ice cream	1 dsp
	few strawberries	

Place all the ingredients in a blender and whizz them until frothy. Serve in a beaker or a tall glass with straws.

Fresh Fruit Salad

F E V Q

Traditional recipe books tell you to put a fruit salad in a sugar syrup. This is quite unnecessary - using fruit juice prevents the fruit from going brown, and the salad tastes beautifully fresh, not cloyingly sweet.

2	apples	2
1	orange	1
25 g	seedless grapes	1 oz
1	pear	1
	such other interesting fruit as available e.g. pineapple, kiwi fruit, apricots, peaches, orange or apple juice	

Wash and cut fruit into equal-sized pieces. There is no need to peel apples or pears unless the skin is bruised and blemished. Put all fruit together in a bowl and stir in enough apple or orange juice to cover.

Serving suggestion: usually served with cream, but yoghurt or fromage frais make suitable substitutes.

This is delicious with home-made ice cream too.

Compote of Dried Fruit in Apple Juice

F V E

The key to a good compote is slow cooking so that the fruit retains its shape, so once you've brought this to a boil make sure it just bubbles very gently.

85 g	dried (unsulphured) apricots	3 oz
85 g	dried apples	3 oz
85 g	dried prunes	3 oz
85 g	raisins	3 oz
400 ml	apple juice	4 floz
5 cm	cinnamon stick	2 inch
	thinly pared rind of lemon	

Put fruit in a bowl and cover with apple juice. Add the cinnamon stick and lemon rind and leave to soak for 12 hours (or overnight). Remove the lemon rind and cut it into thin strips. Put fruit, juice, cinnamon stick and lemon rind into a saucepan. Bring gently to boil and simmer 15 mins.

Serves 4-6.

Serving suggestion: serve hot, or cool completely and serve with yoghurt.

Nutrient	Units	per portn
Energy	Kcals	220.54
Protein	g	2.50
Fat	g	0.44
Carbohydrate	g	55.18

Stewed Fruit Crumble

It is quicker to prepare a crumble than a pie. Apples, rhubarb, gooseberries, plums, fresh apricots all make delicious crumbles. It is best to cook the fruit lightly first.

Wash and peel, cut, core or stone as appropriate 500 g (1 lb) of fruit. Place in a casserole dish with 1 or 2 tablespoons of sweetener if desired. Unrefined sugar or honey or concentrated fruit juice can be used. Add a tablespoon of orange or apple juice, or water, cover with a lid and place in a moderate oven until the fruit has softened (about 30-45 minutes depending on the fruit - the pieces should be soft, but retain their shape). You can also stew fruit gently in a pan on top of the cooker. This is quicker, but the fruit is likely to collapse to a purée (just what you want for a quick Apple Sauce to serve with pork). However be warned that you run a greater risk of losing the moisture as steam, and the fruit may then burn.

Variation: Substitute up to half the flour with a muesli mix.

Crumble Mix

F E V Ch

250 g	wholemeal flour	8 oz
125 g	margarine	4 oz
25-50 g	sesame seeds	1-2 oz
25-50g	unrefined light soft brown sugar	1-2 oz

Rub the ingredients together in a bowl, until they resemble breadcrumbs (just like pastry). Press over lightly cooked fruit and bake in a moderate oven (without a lid) for about 35 minutes.

Serves 4.

Serving suggestion: with custard, cream or ice cream, if such is your family's taste, though a fruit crumble is actually quite nice on its own.

Nutrient	Units	per portn
Energy	Kcals	486.68
Protein	g	9.16
Fat	g	30.50
Carbohydrate	g	46.83

Fruit Pie

Pastry made with 250 g (8 oz) flour (p28-29) will be more than enough to cover a pie. For a small pie plate (up to say 18 cm/7 inch) it will line the plate and cover the pie. A variation to standard pastry is to replace up to 50 g (2 oz) of flour with ground hazel nuts. Some people like to place the lightly cooked fruit in a pie dish, and cover with pastry rolled out to about 0.5 cm (1/4 inch) thickness. Others like to line the plate with pastry, then add the fruit, and cover with a pastry lid. (A sprinkling of semolina over the bottom layer of pastry will help absorb the juices as the pie cooks.) Whichever you do, bake in a moderate to hot oven for 25-35 minutes, until the pastry is lightly browned.

Pie Fillings

Apple pie must be the all-time favourite. You can add a few sultanas and 1/4 tsp cinnamon for a variation on the theme. Apples are also useful to extend a small quantity of other fruit such as blackcurrants, blackberries, cherries, raspberries, and even strawberries. Rhubarb and gooseberries make excellent pies in their own right. Some sweetener in the fruit is usually preferred, but you can reduce it to 1-2 tablespoons of sugar, or use honey or concentrated fruit juice instead.

Fruit Fools

Are easily made by combining equal quantities of yoghurt and stewed puréed fruit of your choice. Sharp fruits such as rhubarb and gooseberries are ideal for this, but may need a little honey or sugar to sweeten. Strawberries and raspberries don't need to be cooked. Just mash them with a wooden spoon, or whizz up in a blender, then push through a sieve to remove the seeds.

Fruit Ices

F E V Ch

Ice lollies are very popular on hot sunny days. To make your own you need some ice lolly moulds, or an ice cube tray will do, if you can acquire some lolly sticks. Use fresh fruit juice, or fruit purée made from mashing and sieving (or whizzing up in a blender) soft fruits with some apple juice, such as strawberries, raspberries, blackberries, and freeze in the moulds. A little honey or golden granulated sugar can be used to sweeten, if the fruit is very sharp. These are very refreshing, healthy and totally lacking artificial flavourings, colourings and preservatives.

Variations:

- Gelatine comes from animal sources. Vegetarians can use agar-agar, which is derived from seaweed, and used in a similar way (about two teaspoons per 600 ml (1 pint) of liquid).
- It is important not to let the gelatine boil. For this reason, you may like to use this alternative method: Place three tablespoons hot water or juice in a bowl, and sprinkle on the gelatine (add the gelatine to the liquid, not the other way round). Allow the gelatine to soften (for about 5 minutes), then place the bowl over a pan of simmering water. Stir gently until the gelatine has completely dissolved, then add the rest of the juice. Put in a bowl or moulds, leave to cool, then put in fridge until set.
- Milk or yoghurt can be substituted for some of the juice. If you whisk it in when the jelly has nearly set, then leave until set, you will have a light frothy mousse-like dessert.
- Use other fruit juices such as a combination of apple juices and excess juices from stewed black berries or raspberries.

GOOD SOURCE

Vitamin C

Nutrient	Units	per portn
Energy	Kcals	53.45
Protein	g	2.74
Fat	g	0.13
Carbohydrate	g	11.00

Fruit Jelly

F E V Ch

You can add pieces of fresh fruit such as bananas, grapes, oranges, cherries, which will give some fibre.

500 ml	orange juice	1 pt
1	sachet powdered gelatine	1

Put three tablespoons of orange juice in a small saucepan and sprinkle on the gelatine. Leave for 5 minutes then dissolve over a gentle heat, without boiling. When the mixture is clear pour in the rest of the juice and mix well. Pour into dishes or moulds and place in fridge to set.

Serves 4.

Variations: Try other ripe fruit in place of banana. The fun is in creating your own varieties. Experiment with cocoa powder or carob, breadcrumbs, chopped nuts, dried fruit, exotic fruit such as lychees and mango, in different combinations. Add flavouring such as vanilla essence, or concentrated fruit juice.

GOOD SOURCE

Vit A (ret eq)   Vitamin B6

Nutrient	Units	per portn
Energy	Kcals	762.08
Protein	g	3.68
Fat	g	68.46
Carbohydrate	g	34.83

Low-Sugar quick-to-prepare Ice Cream

V

Once you've made your own homemade ice-cream you will realize how different it is from commercial varieties, which are mostly air and whipped up vegetable oils and lots of sugar. The beauty of making your own is you can control how sweet it is and really taste the fruit.

1	small carton double cream	1
	juice of 1/2 lemon	
1	ripe banana	1
	a little maple syrup, honey or fruit sugar	

Blend all ingredients in electric blender. Pour into a small tray and freeze. Beat it again after two hours, before it has set, to eliminate crystals.

Serves 1.

Serving suggestion: as homemade ice cream sets quite hard, take it out of the freezer and put in the fridge about twenty minutes before you want to eat it. You can freeze the mixture in ice lolly moulds, as alternative lollies.

Variations:
* White round grain pudding rice is most generally available. Brown round rice can sometimes be obtained from health food shops. You can, if you like, use long grain brown rice. Brown rice will take longer to cook, and may need extra liquid. It will have a more chewy texture. Flaked rice cooks more quickly. Tapioca can be cooked in the same way.
* If your family doesn't like a skin on a baked rice pudding, try using skimmed milk, and about two tablespoons of water.
* Optional extras to add are: 25 g (1 oz) raisins, and/or grated lemon rind (from a quarter of a lemon will be enough). A sprinkling of grated nutmeg is traditional.

GOOD SOURCE

Vitamin B12

Nutrient	Units	per portn
Energy	Kcals	148.23
Protein	g	5.05
Fat	g	5.07
Carbohydrate	g	21.93

Rice Pudding

V Ch

A very easy pudding to prepare and leave to look after itself until you are ready for it.

50 g	rice	2 oz
600 ml	milk	1 pt
25 g	golden granulated sugar	1 oz

Put all ingredients together.

Method 1. Use a double saucepan and cook gently over boiling water, stirring from time to time, until the rice is soft and creamy and has absorbed most of the milk (at least 30 minutes).

Method 2. Use a greased shallow dish and place in low oven for at least two hours.

Remember that the secret of a creamy rice pudding is long slow cooking with gentle heat. If using the oven method, you can place the dish at the very bottom of a moderate oven, while cooking a casserole or joint.

Serves 4.

Baked Semolina

V Ch

Semolina, which is simply coarsely ground Durum wheat, makes a simple but nutritious pudding but being homemade, very different from what you may have had in school days!

600 ml	milk	1 pt
25 g	semolina	1 oz
25 g	golden granulated sugar	1 oz
1	egg	1

Warm the milk in a saucepan over a gentle heat. Just before it reaches boiling point, sprinkle in the semolina and sugar, and stir gently over the heat until it thickens (about 7 minutes). Take off the heat, and while it is cooling, separate the egg. Stir the egg yolk into the semolina. Whisk the egg white until stiff, fold it into the semolina, turn mixture into a greased dish and brown in moderate oven.

Serves 4.

Serving suggestion: try this with jam or stewed apples or raisins.

GOOD SOURCE

Vitamin B12

Nutrient	Units	per portn
Energy	Kcals	147.37
Protein	g	6.23
Fat	g	6.34
Carbohydrate	g	17.41

Junket

Ch

This old favourite may be liked by children who find yoghurt too sharp. It may also tempt those with sore throats. You can serve it with jam.

600 ml	milk	1 pt
1 tbsp	demerara sugar	1 tbsp
1 tsp	liquid rennet (not easy to get hold of - try health food shops)	1 tsp

Gently heat milk until just warm to the finger. Remove from heat and stir in sugar. Add rennet stirring gently. Pour into dishes and leave undisturbed to set (but do not cool too rapidly).

Serves 4.

GOOD SOURCE

Vitamin B12

Nutrient	Units	per portn
Energy	Kcals	100.00
Protein	g	4.04
Fat	g	4.88
Carbohydrate	g	10.62

Variation: Instead of vanilla, add a little grated lemon rind.

Impossible Pie

V

You'll see why this pudding got its name when you serve it.

4	eggs	4
50 g	butter or margarine	2 oz
125-175 g	golden granulated sugar according to taste	4-6 oz
60 g	plain flour (white or wholemeal)	2-3 oz
¼ tsp	salt (optional)	¼ tsp
¼ tsp	baking powder	¼ tsp
600 ml	milk	1 pt
125 g	dessicated coconut	4 oz
1 tsp	vanilla (optional)	1 tsp

Place all ingredients in blender at one time and blend until mixed together. Pour into a buttered 25 cm (10 inch) pie dish, or loose bottom cake tin. Bake in a moderate oven for one hour. When done, crust will be on the bottom, custard in the middle, and coconut on top - right where they belong. Amazing !
Serves 4.

GOOD SOURCE

Fibre	Vitamin B12
Vit A (ret eq)	Calcium
Riboflavin	

Nutrient	Units	per portn
Energy	Kcals	619.82
Protein	g	13.69
Fat	g	40.06
Carbohydrate	g	54.55

Cakes and Bakes

for Dessert or Tea-Time

HEALTHIER SPONGE

SUGARLESS CARROT CAKE

YOGHURT CAKE

BARA BRITH

HARVEST FRUIT LOAF

GRANARY FRUIT BREAD

BANANA LOAF

FRESH APPLE CAKE

CUT AND COME AGAIN CAKE

*NOT-TOO-NAUGHTY
CHOCOLATE CAKE*

CHOCOLATE ROULADE

*TOPPINGS AND
FILLINGS FOR CAKES*

BASIC SCONES

BANANA ROCK BUNS

ORANGE DATE BUNS

OATMEAL DIGESTIVE BISCUITS

OATCAKES

FLAPJACKS

CHOCOLATE ORANGE BARS

Large cakes can be served as dessert after a meal, or to fill the hunger gap in between. They can be good for you, with lots of fresh or dried fruit, sunflower oil instead of butter, and the sugar content reduced. Some of these recipes are of the old fashioned "farmhouse" style, others are "healthy" ideas which work.

The texture of loaves and cakes is lightened in one or more of several ways: incorporating lots of air by beating fat and sugar together, or beating eggs; use of raising agents such as baking powder or bicarbonate of soda; use of yeast, when the dough requires vigorous kneading and warmth. Cakes made with oil, or lots of fruit may be stickier or moister than you are used to, but no less tasty for that.

Tips

Confidence in baking cakes, and knowing the right consistency for the kind of cake you are making, comes with practice. But unless you have burned it, or brought it out of the oven far too soon, whatever you make is likely to be edible. Don't be nervous of having a go.

- Always line the bottom of cake tins with greaseproof paper cut to size (the children can prepare a pile of these for you one wet afternoon), and grease the sides with margarine or oil.
- Preheat the oven - in other words, turn it on to the right temperature before you start mixing.
- To test if a cake is done
  - are the sides shrinking away from the tin ?
  - does the top spring back when pressed ?
  - does a skewer poked into the centre come out clean ?
  If the answer to all three is yes, it's ready.
- Most cakes are best removed from the tin immediately and cooled on a wire rack.

Do pay attention to the proportions of fat, eggs and flour in these recipes. A too dry or too wet mixture will affect results.

Tip: When spooning honey, golden syrup or malt extract for cakes and biscuits dip the spoon in boiling water first, it helps the syrup to pour off easily.

Healthier Sponge
(standard ingredients given in brackets)

V

The added ingredients (fruit, nuts, spices) can be varied to suit your taste. Once you are confident with a recipe, however, you can adapt it. To illustrate, here is a variation of the standard Victorian sponge recipe found in most books.

50 g	stoned dates, chopped small	2 oz
4 tbsp	orange juice	4 tbsp
1 dsp	malt extract	1 dsp
175 g	butter or margarine (180 g butter)	6 oz
125 g	unrefined light muscovado sugar (175g/6oz caster sugar)	4 oz
3	eggs	3
175 g	self-raising wholemeal flour, or half wholemeal and half white self-raising flour	6 oz
25 g	soya flour	1 oz
1 dsp	cocoa or carob powder	1 dsp

Place the dates, orange juice and malt extract in a saucepan, bring to boil, simmer gently for 3 - 5 minutes, then switch off heat and leave to soak. This will soften the dates. Cream the margarine and sugar together until light and fluffy. Beat the eggs in a separate bowl, then beat them gradually into the margarine and sugar. If the mixture is curdling, add a tablespoon of the sieved flour. Fold in the remainder of the sieved flours and cocoa, if using. ("Fold" means gently cutting the flour into the mixture with a metal spoon, so as not to knock out the air which has been beaten in.) Mash the dates and orange juice with a wooden spoon, and stir into the cake mixture. It should be a soft dropping consistency. A little extra orange juice can be added if necessary. Turn the mixture into a 20-23 cm (8-9 inch) round cake tin and bake in a moderate oven. Test after 35 minutes.

Makes 12 slices.

The recipe given above is ideal for a birthday cake, and can be filled and iced as you prefer. See p144 for ideas.

GOOD SOURCE

Vit A (ret eq)

Nutrient	Units	per portn
Energy	Kcals	241.59
Protein	g	4.86
Fat	g	14.28
Carbohydrate	g	24.99

Variations: Substitute honey for malt extract or use grated apple instead of grated carrot.

Sugarless Carrot Cake

V Ch

Carrot cakes are always popular for everyday eating and perhaps including in a lunch box. If you want to make it more special you could top it with a little orange or lemon icing.

50 g	dates, chopped small	2 oz
80 g	raw grated carrot	3 oz
4 tbsp	natural apple juice	4 tbsp
80 g	butter or margarine	3 oz
1 dsp	malt extract	1 dsp
175 g	self-raising wholemeal flour	6 oz
1 tsp	ground cinnamon	1 tsp
	freshly grated nutmeg	
2	eggs, beaten	2
50 g	raisins	2 oz
50 g	sultanas	2 oz

Soak dates and grated carrot in the apple juice. Cream the butter with the malt extract until very soft and light. Sieve the flour with cinnamon and nutmeg. Beat the eggs in a separate bowl. Gradually beat flour and egg mixtures into the butter. (The mixture should be a little stiffer than the average cake mixture.) Mix in carrots, fruit and juice, turn mixture into greased and lined 18 cm (7 inch) cake tin and smooth top. Bake for about 1 hour 45 minutes in a low - moderate oven. Cool on wire rack.

Makes 12 slices.

GOOD SOURCE

Vit A (ret eq)

Nutrient	Units	per portn
Energy	Kcals	150.26
Protein	g	3.40
Fat	g	6.84
Carbohydrate	g	20.03

Variation: Add 25-50 g (1-2 oz) sultanas.

Yoghurt Cake

V

This is a very easy low cholesterol cake.
Using a 100 g (4 oz) yoghurt carton as a measure:

1	carton each of natural yoghurt	1
	unrefined golden granulated or light muscovado sugar	
	sunflower oil	
2	cartons self-raising wholemeal flour	2
1	beaten egg	1

Beat all the ingredients together and place in greased loaf tin. Bake in a moderate oven (180°C, 350°F, gas mark 4) for about 45 minutes - 1 hour, until firm to touch.

Makes 14 slices.

Serving suggestion: try serving it warm with custard.

Nutrient	Units	per portn
Energy	Kcals	215.79
Protein	g	3.76
Fat	g	11.67
Carbohydrate	g	25.55

Tip: If muscovado sugar is at all dry or lumpy, rub it into flour with fingers, breaking down the lumps.

Bara Brith

V Ch

A traditional Welsh fruit cake

300 ml	cold tea or orange juice	½ pt
350 g	sultanas	12 oz
350 g	wholemeal flour	12 oz
2-3 tsp	baking powder	2-3 tsp
2 tsp	mixed spice	2 tsp
	pinch salt	
225 g	dark muscovado sugar	8 oz
2	eggs	2

   Soak the sultanas in the cold tea or orange juice, overnight if possible. Sieve together the flour, baking powder, spice and salt. Add the sugar and sultanas with the tea or juice. Beat eggs and add to the mixture, with a little milk or orange juice if needed to give a soft dropping consistency. Using the centre of a moderate oven, bake in lined loaf tin for approximately 1 hour or until firm to touch. Do line the tin, otherwise you will find it hard to get the loaf out in one piece.

Makes 14 slices.

Nutrient	Units	per portn
Energy	Kcals	235.98
Protein	g	5.01
Fat	g	1.48
Carbohydrate	g	54.03

Variations:
- Try adding nuts, sunflower seeds, or cherries to replace some of the dried fruit.
- Using dark muscovado sugar, and/or melting a tablespoon of blackstrap molasses, or black treacle or malt extract with the butter or margarine will give a richer cake.

Nutrient	Units	per portn
Energy	Kcals	188.13
Protein	g	3.68
Fat	g	8.86
Carbohydrate	g	25.00

Harvest Fruit Loaf

V Ch

This moist fruit cake couldn't be easier to make, there is no lengthy beating or creaming so it's ideal when you're short of time but want to have a cake to serve.

125 g	butter or margarine	4 oz
125 g	golden granulated or light muscovado sugar	4 oz
75 g	mixed dried fruit	3 oz
225 g	self-raising wholemeal flour	8 oz
1 tsp	mixed spice	1 tsp
150 ml	milk	1/4 pt
2	eggs, beaten	2

Melt the butter or margarine. Mix all dry ingredients together in a bowl, add the melted margarine, milk and beaten eggs and stir together to make a soft consistency. Bake in a greased and lined 2lb loaf tin at 160°C, 325°F, gas mark 3 for 1 1/2 - 1 3/4 hours. Leave in tin for 10 minutes before turning out to cool on wire tray.

Makes 14 slices.

Variation: If you are short of time, just prove once in the tins before baking.

Granary Fruit Bread

F E V Ch

This is a substantial bread, rather than a cake. Slices can be eaten with butter, toasted if you like. Although the instructions look long and complicated, it is basically bread with dried fruit added, and just as easy to make.

675 g	granary flour	1¼ lb
1 tsp	salt	1 tsp
50 g	dark soft brown sugar	2 oz
125-225g	dried fruits, seeds or nuts (choose from raisins, sultanas, currants, prunes, apricots, dates, chopped nuts, sunflower or pumpkin seeds)	4-8 oz
1	sachet easy blend yeast	1
425 ml	hand hot water	¾ pt
1 tbsp	malt extract	1 tbsp
2 tbsp	sunflower oil	2 tbsp

Bring flour into warm place for an hour or so. Chop large dried fruit such as apricots. Add all dry ingredients to the flour, including the fruit. Sprinkle in the dry yeast, and stir in. Make a well in centre. In a jug mix the water, malt extract and oil, and pour into the flour mixture. With one hand gradually draw together flour and liquid until a soft dough is produced. More water may be added if necessary. Turn the dough onto a worktop and knead until it becomes slightly firmer and silky to touch. Put back in bowl. Pour about a teaspoon of oil into the palm of your hand and spread over the ball of dough to prevent it drying out. Cover loosely with polythene bag or cling film and put in warm place to prove.

When the dough has doubled in volume turn out onto the worktop again and gently knead it to knock down. Divide the dough into two, shape into rolls and put in two 1lb greased loaf tins. Oil the tops of the loaves and cover with polythene bags. Allow to rise until the dough is rounded over the top of the tins. Remove polythene bag and bake in hot oven for 30 minutes or until the loaves sound hollow when tapped on the bottom.

Makes 14 slices per loaf.

Nutrient	Units	per portn
Energy	Kcals	114.99
Protein	g	3.15
Fat	g	1.27
Carbohydrate	g	24.24

Variations:
- The cinnamon can be omitted altogether, or half replaced with ½ tsp ground ginger.
- 50 g (2 oz) chopped walnuts can be added with the raisins. This loaf keeps well wrapped in foil. It also freezes well.

Nutrient	Units	per portn
Energy	Kcals	172.89
Protein	g	3.58
Fat	g	6.20
Carbohydrate	g	27.39

Banana Loaf

V Ch

This cake is perfect for using up those bananas in the fruit bowl that have gone a bit too mushy and brown to eat.

225 g	self-raising wholemeal flour	8 oz
1 tsp	baking powder	1 tsp
1 tsp	cinnamon	1 tsp
100-125 g	light muscovado sugar or clear honey	4 oz
2	eggs	2
85 g	melted butter or margarine or sunflower oil	3 oz
2-3	ripe bananas	2-3
100-125 g	raisins or sultanas	3-4 oz

Mix together the dry ingredients. Beat the eggs with melted butter or oil, together with honey if using instead of sugar. Mash the bananas and add to the egg mixture. (A food processor can be used to beat the eggs, butter, honey and bananas). Stir the egg/banana mixture into the flour. Do not over process at this stage. Add a little hot water if necessary to give a soft dropping consistency. Mix in the raisins or sultanas. Turn into a greased and lined 2lb loaf tin and bake in a moderate oven for about 50 minutes - 1 hour. Cool the loaf in the tin before turning out.

Makes 14 slices.

Variations:
- Replace one of the apples with grated carrot.
- Adjust the spices to suit your taste.
- Replace some or all of the nuts with dessicated coconut.

Fresh Apple Cake

V

You can use cooking or eating apples for this recipe, either will do but you will get a slightly different texture of cake since eating apples hold their shape more when cooked. In any case there will be no difference in the amount of vitamin A.

3	apples, peeled and chopped or grated	3
250 g	unrefined golden granulated or light muscovado sugar	8 oz
200 ml	oil	7 floz
3	eggs	3
225 g	self-raising flour	8 oz
1 tsp	ground cinnamon	1 tsp
½ tsp	grated nutmeg	½ tsp
125 g	walnuts	4 oz
125 g	raisins	4 oz
1 tsp	vanilla (optional)	1 tsp

Grease and line two 20-23 cm (8-9 inch) cake tins. Place chopped or grated apple in bowl, add sugar and mix. Beat in oil and eggs with a wooden spoon. Sift dry ingredients together, add to cake mixture. Stir in nuts, raisins and vanilla. Pour into prepared tins. Bake for 55 minutes in a moderate oven.

Makes 12 slices.

Nutrient	Units	per portn
Energy	Kcals	391.65
Protein	g	5.26
Fat	g	21.07
Carbohydrate	g	48.26

Variation: Double the mixture and use half to make rock cakes. Place rough spoonfuls of the mixture on to a greased baking sheet, and bake for about 20 minutes.

Cut and Come Again Cake

V

If you find that dried fruit or nuts settle at the bottom when you make cakes it will be because the mixture is not thick enough to hold them, so if you toss nuts, raisins and other chopped fruit in flour it will help keep them suspended in the cake mixture.

250 g	self-raising wholemeal flour (or use half white, half wholemeal)	8 oz
pinch	salt	pinch
2 tsp	mixed spice	2 tsp
125 g	butter or margarine	4 oz
90 g	golden granulated sugar	3 oz
175 g	mixed dried fruit	6 oz
1 tsp	grated orange or lemon rind	1 tsp
1	egg plus milk and water to make up to150 ml (1/4 pt)	1

Grease and line a 20 cm (8 inch) round cake tin. Sieve the flour, with salt and spice. Add fat and rub in until mixture resembles fine breadcrumbs. Stir in sugar, fruit and rind. Make a well in the centre and add beaten egg and milk. Mix well. Place mixture into tin and bake in moderate oven for approx 1 1/4 hours.

Makes 12 slices.

Nutrient	Units	per portn
Energy	Kcals	226.19
Protein	g	3.75
Fat	g	9.68
Carbohydrate	g	33.11

Not-Too-Naughty Chocolate Cake

E V

This is a rich looking and tasting cake which actually has less fat and sugar proportionately than most sponge cakes.

115 g	butter or margarine	4 oz
150 ml	water	¼ pt
2 tbsp	syrup or blackstrap molasses	2 tbsp
280 g	self-raising flour, half wholemeal, half white	10 oz
25 g	soya flour	1 oz
75 g	light or dark muscovado sugar	3 oz
½ tsp	salt	½ tsp
3 tbsp	carob or cocoa powder	3 tbsp
1 tsp	bicarbonate of soda	1 tsp

Melt butter or margarine over a low heat with the water and syrup. Allow to cool. Mix flour, sugar, salt, carob or cocoa powder and bicarbonate of soda together in a bowl. Pour the wet ingredients into the dry, and stir to mix. Turn into a greased and lined 18 cm (7 inch) square tin or loose bottom round tin. Bake in moderate oven for ¾ - 1 hour. Cool on wire tray.

Makes 12 slices.

Serving suggestion: fill "Black Forest Gateau" style with a cherry or blackcurrant jam or sauce (simply made by lightly stewing fresh fruit with a little honey), fresh fruit and cream or cream substitute such as crème fraîche, or even ice cream. The top may be quite crusty, if so, a dusting of icing sugar will be best.

Nutrient	Units	per portn
Energy	Kcals	198.05
Protein	g	4.25
Fat	g	9.19
Carbohydrate	g	26.24

Tip: If you don't have castor sugar, you can make some by whizzing up some ordinary granulated sugar in a food processor or clean coffee grinder. But don't whiz for too long, or you'll end up with icing sugar.

Chocolate Roulade

A special treat to impress, and again not too unhealthy.

3	eggs	3
90 g	golden granulated or castor sugar	3 oz
90 g	plain wholemeal flour	3 oz
3 tbsp	cocoa or carob powder, sieved	3 tbsp
1 tbsp	castor sugar	1 tbsp
225 g	fromage frais	8 oz
2 tbsp	icing sugar	2 tbsp
125 g	fresh fruit e.g. morello cherries, raspberries	4 oz

Whisk eggs and sugar until thick. Add sifted flour and cocoa and carefully fold in. Pour into a greased and lined 30 cm x 20 cm (12 inch x 8 inch) swiss roll tin. Bake at 200°C, 400°F, gas mark 6 for 8 - 10 minutes, until sponge springs back when pressed in centre. Wring out a clean tea towel in hot water and lay on worktop. Place a sheet of greaseproof paper on top, sprinkle with castor sugar. Turn sponge onto paper, remove lining paper and trim crisp edges from long sides. Roll up sponge with sugared paper inside, remove cloth and place on wire rack to cool. Mix fromage frais and icing sugar, stir in fruit. Unroll cooled sponge, remove paper, spread with filling and roll up again.

Makes 16 slices.

Nutrient	Units	per portn
Energy	Kcals	89.95
Protein	g	3.26
Fat	g	2.55
Carbohydrate	g	14.37

TOPPINGS AND FILLINGS FOR CAKES

Sponge cakes and small buns often seem to need a filling or topping. Butter cream and glacé, or fondant icing use a lot of icing sugar, and butter or margarine.

For low-fat healthier options try fruity cake fillings: stewed apple or other fruit can be used, or soft fruit such as strawberries, mashed to a purée - a good way of using thawed frozen strawberries which don't hold their texture. Many tinned fruits are now available without added sugar. Drained tinned apricots, puréed, make a particularly good cake filling.

If you are introducing less sweet cakes to your family, it might help if they have just a sprinkling of dry icing sugar on top. This uses far less than the usual glacé icing. You could use the children's stencil set to dust on interesting designs - or why not let the children do it themselves?

If you do want to make glacé icing, to two tablespoons of icing sugar, gradually stir in some orange juice, a few drops at a time. Use a teaspoon to drizzle over small buns.

Whipped cream may be high in fat, but at least it has no sugar. Try experimenting with thick greek yoghurt, and crème fraîche, or fromage frais, as alternatives.

FINGER BARS AND SNACKS

These provide picnic and lunch box snacks. They are also good for serving at LLL meetings.

Basic Scones

V Ch

225 g	self-raising wholemeal flour, or half white and half wholemeal if you prefer	8 oz
½ tsp	salt	½ tsp
1 tsp	baking powder	1 tsp
75 g	butter or margarine	3 oz
	milk to mix (up to 150 ml/¼ pt)	

Variations:

• Cheese - add 25 g (1 oz) grated cheese plus 1 dsp grated Parmesan and a pinch mustard powder if liked.

• Fruit - add 25 g (1 oz) raisins or sultanas, and 25 g (1 oz) golden granulated sugar if wished.

• Date - chop 25 g (1 oz) dates into small pieces, and soak in milk before adding to flour.

• Some people use a beaten egg and milk to make the dough.

• Buttermilk or yoghurt can be used instead of the milk to mix the dough.

Nutrient	Units	per Scone
Energy	Kcals	137.72
Protein	g	2.25
Fat	g	7.46
Carbohydrate	g	16.41

Rub butter into flour. Add extra ingredients (see Variations below). Stir in enough milk to make a light dough. It needs to be a little wetter and softer than pastry, without being sticky. Handle lightly. Roll the dough out on a floured surface to 2 cm (1/2 inch) thickness and either cut into rounds and place on a greased baking sheet (children like to help with this), or if you are in a hurry, simply press into a shallow rectangular baking tin and cut into bars. Bake in hot oven for about 15 minutes (rounds) or 25 minutes (bars). Cool on wire tray.

Makes 12.

Banana Rock Buns

V Ch

This is another recipe which is useful for using up those soft, mushy bananas, but if you have more than you will use for this recipe you can always freeze them. Mash them with a teaspoon of lemon juice for each banana and freeze in a container for up to six months.

225 g	self-raising wholemeal flour	8 oz
1 tsp	baking powder	1 tsp
75 g	butter or margarine	3 oz
1 tbsp	light muscovado sugar	1 tbsp
50 g	sultanas	2 oz
2	bananas	2
1 tsp	juice and a little grated lemon rind	1 tsp
1	egg	1

Nutrient	Units	per Bun
Energy	Kcals	143.24
Protein	g	3.28
Fat	g	6.04
Carbohydrate	g	20.21

Sieve flour and baking powder together. Rub in butter or margarine. Stir in sugar and fruit. Mash the bananas with the lemon juice, rind and egg. Add to flour mixture and stir together, using a little milk if needed to make a soft mixture. Place in spoonfuls on greased baking sheet and bake for 15 - 20 minutes in a hot oven. Cool on wire tray.

Makes 12.

Variations: Use 175 g (6 oz) wholemeal flour and 50 g (2 oz) soya flour. Chopped nuts can also be added. 1 tbsp honey or light muscovado sugar can be added for extra sweetness.

Nutrient	Units	per Bun
Energy	Kcals	203.44
Protein	g	3.64
Fat	g	11.35
Carbohydrate	g	23.14

Orange Date Buns

V

In America these would be called muffins.

100 g	dates chopped small	4 oz
200 ml	orange juice	7 floz
225 g	self-raising wholemeal flour	8 oz
1 tsp	baking powder	1 tsp
1	egg	1
150 ml	sunflower oil	¼ pt
1 tbsp	malt extract	1 tbsp

You will need a twelve cup bun tray. Line each cup with a paper bun case. If you don't, they will stick to the tin and be difficult to get out.

Put dates and orange juice in saucepan, bring to boil, simmer for 3 - 5 minutes, turn off heat and leave to soak. Sieve together flour and baking powder. Beat together the egg, oil, and malt extract. Stir into flour, and add dates and juice. Stir just until all ingredients are mixed. Divide mixture between bun cases and bake in hot oven for about 15 minutes.

Makes 12.

Oatmeal Digestive Biscuits

V Ch

To make perfect biscuits use cold butter or margarine and once the flour is added don't handle or mix the dough too much.

225 g	medium oatmeal	8 oz
225 g	plain wholemeal flour	8 oz
175 g	butter or margarine	6 oz
75 g	golden granulated sugar	3 oz
	pinch salt	
	pinch bicarbonate of soda	
1	egg, beaten	1

Nutrient	Units	per Biscuit
Energy	Kcals	154.96
Protein	g	2.92
Fat	g	8.17
Carbohydrate	g	18.61

Rub fat into flour and oatmeal. Add all other ingredients and mix until they bind. Mould the dough into a sausage shape about 8 cm (3 inch) in diameter and with a sharp knife slice into biscuits. If you find it hard to get the sausage to hold its shape, try chilling it in fridge for half a hour. Alternatively, roll out to 5 mm (¼ inch) thickness, and cut out rounds, or shape rounds with hands. Bake 15-20 minutes in a moderate oven until crisp and just colouring slightly.

Makes 24.

Oatcakes
F V Ch

These traditional Scottish oatcakes can be served warm or cold and they are delicious with cheese and celery or butter and jam and are ideal for children to snack on.

125 g	medium oatmeal	4 oz
½ tsp	salt	½ tsp
½ tsp	bicarbonate of soda	½ tsp
2 tsp	oil	2 tsp
	boiling water	

Nutrient	Units	per Biscuit
Energy	Kcals	69.40
Protein	g	1.94
Fat	g	2.11
Carbohydrate	g	11.38

Mix the oats with the salt and bicarbonate of soda, then add the oil and sufficient boiling water to make a soft dough. Knead lightly on a floured surface, then roll out thinly into an 20 cm (8 inch) circle. Cut the round into 8 wedges. The oatcakes can either be baked in the oven on a greased baking sheet at 200°C (400°F) gas mark 6 for 15-20 minutes or baked in a heavy oiled frying pan. Make sure the pan is really hot (test by dropping in a few oats which should turn brown instantly). Bake the oatcakes for 3-4 minutes on each side until lightly browned. These oatcakes should be crisp, browned and curling up at the edges. Leave to cool.

Makes 8.

Variations:

• 75 g (2-3 oz) dessicated coconut may be added, or chopped dried fruit such as apricots, dates, raisins, or sunflower or sesame seeds. Flapjacks are high in fat and sugar, so the extras will add to their nutritional value, and enable the sugar to be reduced by up to 50 g (2 oz), if you prefer. Keep the syrup in, though, it's the stickiness that makes flapjacks what they are.

• Malt extract can be used instead of syrup with good results.

Nutrient	Units	per Biscuit
Energy	Kcals	192.21
Protein	g	2.44
Fat	g	11.44
Carbohydrate	g	21.21

Flapjacks

E V Ch

These make a good addition to a lunch box, picnic or the school fete.

225 g	butter or margarine	8 oz
100 g	unrefined demerara sugar	4 oz
2 tbsp	golden syrup	2 tbsp
100 g	wholemeal flour	4 oz
225 g	rolled oats	8 oz

Melt butter, sugar and syrup in a saucepan. Stir in oats and flour. When well coated, spread evenly in a greased shallow tin. Bake in moderate oven for 25 - 30 minutes.

Makes 20.

Chocolate Orange Bars
E V Ch

This recipe is so simple that it's one the children could help with and is a good one for school's cookery competitions, or summer fairs.

100 g	self-raising wholemeal flour	4 oz
75 g	quick porridge oats	3 oz
50 g	golden granulated or light muscovado sugar	2 oz
2 tbsp	cocoa powder	2 tbsp
1 tsp	grated orange rind	1 tsp
	pinch salt	
100 g	butter or margarine	4 oz

Mix dry ingredients together in a bowl. Melt butter or margarine and stir into dry ingredients. When they are well mixed, press mixture into a 18 cm (7 inch) square greased and lined tin. Bake in moderate oven for about 30 minutes.

Serving suggestion: dust with icing sugar, or coat with a glacé icing made with 50-75 g (2-3 oz) icing sugar and orange juice, or cover with melted orange/chocolate flavour cooking chocolate, (or organic chocolate).

Makes 16.

Nutrient	Units	per Bar
Energy	Kcals	127.48
Protein	g	2.17
Fat	g	7.51
Carbohydrate	g	13.68

DIY
(Or things to do when you are feeling adventurous)

MUESLI

GRANOLA

FRUIT SPREAD

FRUIT BUTTER

APPLE (NO ADDED SUGAR)
MINCEMEAT

YOGHURT IDEAS

YOGHURT CHEESE

RAISED PIE WITH A HOT
WATER CRUST

LEMON BARLEY

NAN BREAD

Muesli

F E V Q

Muesli is an ideal breakfast cereal. The nuts, seeds, grains and dried fruit are packed full of almost the whole range of unrefined protein, minerals and vitamins. There are plenty of commercial varieties available, though many have added sugar, and such things as whey powder. Making your own may not be much cheaper, but you can customise it to your own family's tastes. It is really very easy, and toddlers can have lots of fun helping to weigh, measure, mix and stir. They might even eat some.

450 g	jumbo or porridge oats (or muesli base mix, available from health food shops)	1 lb
100 g	seeds, such as sunflower, sesame, pumpkin	4 oz
100 g	nuts, such as chopped almonds, hazelnuts, walnuts	4 oz
50 g	wheatgerm, dessicated coconut, brewers yeast	2 oz
140 g	raisins, sultanas	5 oz
100 g	chopped dried fruit, such as dates, apricots, bananas	4 oz

   The proportions given above are only a suggestion - you can vary them to suit yourself. Half the oats could be replaced by other rolled grains such as barley, rye, wheat. Mix altogether and store in a large crock pot or plastic container with a tight fitting lid.

   Serving suggestion: in a bowl with milk. Fresh fruit such as apples, bananas, nectarines and strawberries can be chopped and added. Yoghurt can be used instead of milk. If your children don't take milk, then the muesli can be served with orange juice poured over instead.

GOOD SOURCE

Fibre	Folic acid (T)
Thiamin	Magnesium
Vitamin B6	Iron

Nutrient	Units	per 100g
Energy	Kcals	401.34
Protein	g	12.71
Fat	g	17.57
Carbohydrate	g	51.25

Granola

Granola is a variation of muesli which is toasted in the oven.

Ingredients as for muesli recipe, plus:

100 g	margarine	4 oz
125 ml	water	4 floz
4 tbsp	clear honey	4 tbsp

Put the margarine, water and honey in a large roasting tin and melt in a low oven. Add the muesli cereals, nuts and seeds, stirring to coat. Return to the oven and slowly toast for about an hour, stirring from time to time. Remove from oven and when cool add the dry fruit, and store as muesli.

Serving suggestion: as muesli. It can also be eaten dry as a snack-in-hand. Better than biscuits or crisps.

<u>GOOD SOURCE</u>

Fibre	Folic acid (T)
Thiamin	Magnesium
Vitamin B6	Iron

Nutrient	Units	per 100g
Energy	Kcals	405.30
Protein	g	10.78
Fat	g	21.14
Carbohydrate	g	45.79

Alternative Jam

Homemade jam is lovely. Unfortunately, it is at least 50% added sugar, and the long boiling probably destroys most of the goodness in the fruit. So here are two ways of providing fruity spreads that are a bit healthier.

Fruit Spread

F E V

450 g	any fresh or dried fruit	1 lb

Almost any fresh or dried fruit can be used. Try apricots, apples, prunes, blackberries. Dried fruit needs to be soaked overnight before cooking. The basic system is to cook the fruit with a very little liquid and then sieve or process to obtain a thick purée. For the liquid, you can use fruit juice or water if the fruit is sweet enough. If the fruit is very sharp, a dessertspoon of honey could be added.

Serving suggestion: spread can be used on bread, toast, pancakes, yoghurt and other puddings. Keeps for two weeks in the fridge so make only small quantities.

Wash jars in Milton solution, and dry off in an oven with the heat just turned on. Hot jam into cold jars may cause the jars to crack.

Fruit Butter

F E V Ch

This jam is a cross between a jam and a jelly and a useful way to use windfall apples. It will keep in a cool larder when sealed with jam pot covers. It does contain sugar, but proportionately less than most recipes, is cheap to make if using windfalls and garden or pick-your-own produce, and does not contain the additives of bought jam.

1 kg	apples	2 lb
1 kg	fruit in season, currants, blackberries, plums etc	2 lb
	water and sugar (see method)	

Wash and roughly chop apples, put into a large pan with other fruit and 600 ml (1 pint) water. Cook until fruit is broken down, then sieve into a large bowl which you have previously weighed. Weigh again to calculate weight of pulp. To each 450 g (1 lb) of pulp add 350 g (12 oz) sugar. Return to pan and boil for about 30 minutes until thickened. To test, put a teaspoonful on a plate. If no wet ring appears around the pulp it is ready. Ladle into small sterilised warmed jars and cover with jam pot covers.

Serving suggestion: Line a greased shallow rectangular tin with pastry, spread with mincemeat, and cover with another layer of pastry, brush with milk, sprinkle golden granulated sugar on top, mark into twelve fingers or squares and bake in moderate oven about 30 mins. Cool on wire tray. The top layer can be muesli or a crumble mix instead of pastry.

Apple (no added sugar) Mincemeat

F E V

Mince pies for Christmas is the obvious choice. But why limit them to Christmas? They are good at any time of year.

This quantity makes about 5 kilos (12 jars). If this is too much, or too expensive, reduce quantities to suit. Exact proportions are not critical, so adapt the recipe to your own taste. If you use windfall apples, the cost of this mincemeat is reasonable.

1.5 kg	apples, washed and cored	3 lb
2	oranges, cut up and pips removed	2
1	grapefruit, cut up and pips removed	1
3	lemons, cut up and pips removed	3
1 kg	sultanas	2 lb
750 g	currants	1½ lb
750 g	raisins	1½ lb
750 g	other dried fruit such as dates, apricots, figs	1½ lb
1	nutmeg, grated	1
25 g	each of sesame seeds, sunflower seeds and chopped peanuts, almonds or other nuts	1 oz
1 dsp	salt	1 dsp
1 dsp	mixed spice	1 dsp
250 ml	sunflower oil	½ pt

Wash and cut off skin blemishes from fresh fruit. Cut up and core or remove pips, but leave on skin and peel. Use a food processor to mince all the ingredients then mix them well together with the oil. Some honey could be added if you want it sweeter. It is the sugar in mincemeat that preserves it. As there is no sugar in this version, it is best kept long-term in a freezer in usable quantities. Mincemeat often has alcohol added, it helps preserve it. You may not want it in the mincemeat you give the children, but why not add some brandy and perhaps calvados to a jar or two for the grown-ups?

GOOD SOURCE

Fibre	Calcium
Thiamin	Magnesium
Vitamin B6	Iron
Vitamin C	

Nutrient	Units	per Jar
Energy	Kcals	972.94
Protein	g	9.64
Fat	g	20.00
Carbohydrate	g	199.17

- Yoghurt can be used on muesli instead of milk.
- It is often used in Middle Eastern cooking as a sauce thickener, and as a side dish, with cucumber and mint for example.
- Look back at the Cakes section and you will find a recipe for "Yoghurt Cake" (p135).
- Substitute yoghurt for milk in scone recipes.
- Commercial yoghurts often contain added ingredients, not just sugar, but preservatives, flavourings and stabilisers. Using plain yoghurt, or home-made made, will avoid them.

Yoghurt Ideas

V Ch

If you use a lot of yoghurt, either as desserts, or in cooking, you might like to have a go at making your own. Special yoghurt-making equipment can be bought, but you can manage quite easily without.

1 tbsp	good "live" plain yoghurt	1 tbsp
600 ml	milk	1 pt

Put the milk in a saucepan and bring it gently to almost boiling point. This is when bubbles start to form around the edge, but before the milk starts to rise up the pan. Take the pan off the heat, and leave to cool to blood heat. (This is when you dip your finger in and it feels neither warm nor cold). Now, stir in the yoghurt, then transfer to a wide mouthed flask, and put the lid on, or put into a covered bowl or jar which should be kept in a warm place such as next to the boiler or radiator, or in the airing cupboard. The idea is to keep the milk at the right temperature to enable the yoghurt bacteria to get to work. After a few hours, you have yoghurt. Keep it in the fridge and use as required. Save a spoonful for the next batch.

Serving suggestions: Whether you make your own or buy it from the shop, you can add all sorts of fresh or tinned (in own juice) fruits to make quick desserts. The choice is yours. Try also surprise yoghurt, with dried fruit such as raisins or chopped up dates or apricots. A little honey or molasses can be drizzled in - children enjoy stirring patterns.

Serves 4.

GOOD SOURCE

Calcium

Nutrient	Units	per portn
Energy	Kcals	102.25
Protein	g	5.02
Fat	g	5.99
Carbohydrate	g	7.49

Yoghurt Cheese

It is very easy to go one step further and make your own soft cheese. In fact, it is so easy, toddlers can do it!

	one muslin square, sterilised	
600 ml	homemade or shop bought plain, preferably organic, "live" yoghurt	1 pt
	a sieve	
	a bowl	

Place the sieve over the bowl. Line the sieve with a double layer of muslin. Tip the yoghurt into the muslin, and fold over the corners to cover it. Leave the yoghurt in the fridge overnight to drain. In the morning you will have a bowlful of whey, which discard. In the muslin you will have a soft cheese the consistency of thick whipped cream.

Serving suggestions: delicious as a dip for crackers, breadsticks and sticks of raw salad vegetables. You can add chopped chives or other fresh herbs. It can be served on cheese scones. It can even be a cream substitute for sweet scones with fruit or jam, and a topping for carrot cake.

Variation: Once you have tried the recipe using cooked meats, and discovered it is not so difficult, why not make a game pie using an equivalent quantity of rabbit, pheasant, venison etc. The sausagemeat is essential to bind it all together. The meats need not be pre-cooked, they can be removed from the carcases if necessary, and diced and mixed raw with the sausagemeat. The pie may need longer to bake. Test with a skewer. If the top is browning too quickly, cover it with foil.

Raised Pie with a Hot Water Crust

Enormous pork, chicken and ham, or game pies look very impressive. They are ideal for large family gatherings because they can be made in advance. And they are much easier to prepare than you might think. There are three stages, on consecutive days, none in itself too time-consuming for you. An essential piece of equipment is a spring-release loose-bottom cake tin, about 20 cm (8 inch) in diameter and 6 cm (2½ inch) deep. The recipe assumes you have previously cooked a chicken or turkey and/or ham.

Pie Filling

	stock (see method)	
1	onion	1
1	carrot	1
1	bayleaf	1

Filling

1	large onion	1
2	cloves garlic	2
6-8	juniper berries	6-8
6-8	black peppercorns	6-8
450 g	pork sausagemeat	1 lb
1.5 kg	cooked chicken or turkey and ham	3 lb
	salt and black pepper	
1	sachet gelatine	

Crust

400 g	plain flour	14 oz
½ tsp	salt	½ tsp
90 g	lard or hard white vegetable fat	3 oz
225 ml	water	8 floz
1	egg	1

Day One

Slice one onion and carrot. Make a rich stock by simmering a chicken or turkey carcase with the sliced onion, carrot and bayleaf in water for about two and a half hours. Strain the stock, reduce it to about 300 ml (½ pint), cool and keep in fridge overnight.

While the stock is simmering, cut up the cooked chicken or turkey and ham into bite-sized pieces, chop the remaining onion finely, crush the garlic, and juniper berries. Mix all these ingredients with the sausagemeat, with ¼ tsp salt and some freshly ground black pepper. Leave the meat mixture in the fridge overnight.

Day Two

Best to start this early in the day as the pie needs time to bake and cool.

Line the base and side of your spring-release tin with a double layer of greaseproof paper.

Make the hot water crust. This is very easy. Sieve together the flour and salt. Melt the lard in the water and bring to the boil, then pour onto the flour. Beat the flour and water together and knead to form a soft pliable dough. The dough can be left for up to half an hour, covered with cling film, but must be used whilst still warm.

Keep one quarter of the pastry covered, and roll out the remaining three-quarters to an even round large enough to line the base and sides of the tin. Use a rolling pin to carefully lift the pastry over the tin, and ease it down into the corners, taking care not to break it. Leave the excess folded out over the sides of the tin.

Spoon the meat mixture into the pastry, and press it down gently. Roll out the remaining pastry to form a lid, place it over the pie filling, and seal and trim the edges. Use a skewer to make one small hole in the centre, and four more evenly spaced around the edge. Decorate the pie by crimping the edge between finger and thumb, and using pastry trimmings to make leaf shapes which can be placed to half cover the outer holes. Brush the top with beaten egg.

Bake the pie in a pre-heated hot oven for about half an hour, then reduce to a moderate heat and continue baking for about two and a half hours. To test, insert a skewer through the centre hole. The meat should feel tender.

Remove the pie from the oven and leave to cool.

Later on Day Two (or Day Three)

Skim any fat from the stock. Soak the gelatine in 1-2 tablespoons of water, then warm it gently in the stock until it is dissolved. It is important not to let the stock get too hot, as the gelatine will go stringy. Let the stock cool until it is beginning to set, but can still be poured.

GOOD SOURCE

Thiamin	Vitamin B6
Niacin	Vitamin B12

Nutrient	Units	per portn
Energy	Kcals	619.84
Protein	g	37.57
Fat	g	39.90
Carbohydrate	g	29.50

You can either remove the pie from the tin at this stage, or next day.

Carefully and gradually pour the stock into the pie through the holes. (You may find a small funnel useful for this.) Leave the pie in the fridge overnight.

Day Three (or Day Four)

Remove the pie from the tin and liners if you have not already done so.

Serves 12.

Serving suggestion: with lots of crunchy salads and pickles. This is a very useful way of using turkey and ham after Christmas, to provide something special by New Year.

Lemon Barley

F V E Ch

This is an old fashioned invalid drink. The shop variety has additives you may usually wish to avoid. If your children are suffering from one of those indeterminate bugs and can't eat or drink for twenty-four hours, this might go down well, literally as well as metaphorically! It will provide fluid and glucose from the honey or sugar.

3 tbsp	pearl barley	3 tbsp
1 litre	water	2 pts
2	lemons	2
	honey and/ or sugar to taste	

Rinse the pearl barley. Place in a pan with the water, bring to boil and simmer for 15-20 minutes. Strain the water, add the juice of the two lemons and dissolve honey and/or sugar to taste. Allow to cool.

Serving suggestion: A poorly child might like this warm. Take great care that it is not too hot. It is also very refreshing drunk ice cold.

Variation: While it is still hot dip in a rosehip tea bag and leave for 3-4 minutes. This gives the drink a lovely pink colour, adds a fruitiness to the flavour and additional Vitamin C.

GOOD SOURCE

Vitamin C

Nutrient	Units	per 300ml
Energy	Kcals	91.35
Protein	g	1.68
Fat	g	0.39
Carbohydrate	g	21.62

Nan Bread

Contrary to the principle of keeping the recipes in this book simple, this one for Indian Nan Bread is included because the egg, milk and yoghurt offer greater nutritional value than ordinary bread, it is exciting to make, and superb to eat. It is definitely worth the effort.

Warning: You need a very hot grill and oven and twenty minutes concentrated effort at the end to produce the Nans, as well as someone to supervise the children while you are doing it ! Alternatively, Dad might like to have a go, but don't let him have all the fun !

450 g	plain white flour	1 lb
1 tsp	baking powder	1 tsp
½ tsp	salt	½ tsp
1	sachet easy blend yeast	1
1	100 g (4 oz) carton plain yoghurt	1
1	egg	1
2 tbsp	oil	2 tbsp
150 ml	milk	½ pt
1 tsp	honey	1 tsp

In a large bowl mix the flour, baking powder, salt and yeast - make sure it is the kind that just needs to be added to the flour. In another bowl beat together lightly the yoghurt, egg and oil. Bring the milk to blood heat and dissolve the honey in it. Test the milk by dipping in a finger. If it feels neither hot nor cold, it is the right temperature. Add the milk to the flour, followed by the yoghurt etc. Mix to form a dough. It will be quite wet and sticky.

Turn onto a floured board and knead for ten minutes.

Roll the dough in a little oil, then leave in large bowl to prove, covered with cling film.

After about an hour, the dough will have doubled in bulk.

Pre-heat both oven and grill to very hot. Put a flat baking sheet in the oven to get very hot too.

This is the hectic bit, and needs all your concentration.

Turn out the dough, knock it down and knead again for a couple of minutes, then divide into eight pieces. Work with two at a time, covering the rest with cling film until you are ready for them.

Roll out two pieces of dough to oval shapes, like pitta bread. Take the baking sheet out of the oven, and slap the Nans onto it. Return to very hot oven for 3 minutes - during which you can be rolling out the next two. They will begin to rise. Then remove baking sheet from oven and flash under grill about three inches away from the heat. The Nans will puff up spectacularly, and begin to brown. Remove from heat, and wrap in clean tea towel to keep warm until the rest are done.

Serving suggestion: accompany any spicy curry, stew or bean dish. But, whatever you serve it with, it is essential that the rest of the meal can look after itself while you are making the Nans. This is one recipe where white flour is the best choice. Up to a quarter wholemeal is fine, but more than that may make the dough too heavy.

Nutrient	Units	per portn
Energy	Kcals	274.11
Protein	g	8.39
Fat	g	5.12
Carbohydrate	g	51.79

Appendix

CHOKING - what to do if the worst should happen

If a piece of food goes down the wrong way, mostly people manage to cough it up, with no harm done. Occasionally, something can get lodged in the wind pipe, making it impossible to breathe. This is why it is important to supervise babies and young children when they are eating, or experimenting with food items. It is natural that they put things in their mouths, that is how they first explore the world, and learn to eat. They have a very good reflex against swallowing things the wrong way, and **THE CHANCES ARE IT WILL NEVER HAPPEN**. But if it does, and it is obvious that your baby or child can't breathe, this is what the Royal Life Saving Society UK says you should do:

Babies: Lift the baby upside down by the legs, or face down along your thigh or forearm, so that the head is lower than the chest. Give five sharp slaps on the back. If this fails to remove the obstruction, turn him on his back, lay on a firm surface and give five chest thrusts at the bottom of the rib cage, using two fingers. If this fails, check the mouth for any apparent obstruction, clear the airway and attempt one mouth-to-mouth-and-nose ventilation. Call/phone for help. If air cannot be blown in because of continuing obstruction repeat the whole sequence of 5 back slaps followed by 5 chest thrusts, if necessary.

Children: Lean the child forward, either sitting or standing, or on his side, if lying down, and give five back slaps. If this fails, turn him on his back, lay him on a firm surface and give five chest thrusts, using the heel of one hand. If this fails, check the mouth for any obstructions, clear the airway and attempt mouth-to-mouth or mouth-to-mouth-and-nose ventilation. If this fails, give five more back slaps, then five abdominal thrusts, using the heel of one hand, then open airway and ventilate as before. Call/phone for help. Repeat the whole sequence if necessary.

In every case the aim should be to relieve the obstruction with each slap or thrust rather than necessarily to give all five.

THIS IS SIMPLY AN OUTLINE OF THE PROCEDURE. MORE INFORMATION ABOUT RESUSCITATION CAN BE FOUND IN THE RLSS UK BOOK LIFE SUPPORT - OR EVEN BETTER, ATTEND A LIFE SUPPORT CLASS.

INDEX

Useful Addresses

The Soil Association

86 Colston Street
Bristol BS1 5BB
Tel 0117 929 0661, fax 0117 925 2504

They have a mail order catalogue and produce a number of useful booklets, especially their Directory of Farm Shops and Box Schemes, listing outlets for organic fruit and vegetables.

'Q' Guild Limited

PO Box 44
Winterhill House
Snowden Drive, Winterhill, Milton Keynes MK6 1AX
Tel 01908 235018, fax 01908 609825

This is the Guild for Progressive Independent Meat Retailers. They produce a list of all their members throughout the country, most of which sell free-range and organic meat.

Berrydales Special Diet News

Berrydale House
5 Lawn Road, London NW3 2XS
Tel 0171 722 2866, fax 0171 722 7685

This company makes and distributes, by mail order, dairy free, cocoa free, sugar free and diabetic chocolates and produces a quarterly magazine devoted to special dietary problems, allergies and food intolerance. Each issue includes dairy, gluten and egg free, low fat and no added sugar recipes.

The Coeliac Society

PO Box 220
High Wycombe, Bucks HP11 2HY
Tel 01494 437278

The Society publishes a number of helpful booklets and recipe collections for those who are allergic to or sensitive to gluten.

The Food Commission (UK) Ltd

3rd Floor, 5-11 Worship Street
London EC2A 2BH
Tel 0171 628 7774, fax 0171 628 0817

The Food Commission is a national non-profit organization which campaigns for the right to safe, wholesome food. It receives no subsidy from the government, the food industry or advertising. It produces a quarterly magazine and booklets with information on food and food issues.

ABOUT LA LECHE LEAGUE (GREAT BRITAIN)

What La Leche League believes about nutrition
- breastmilk is the superior infant food.
- for the healthy full-term baby breastmilk is the only food necessary until baby shows signs of needing solids about the middle of the first year after birth.
- good nutrition means eating a well-balanced and varied diet of foods in as close to their natural state as possible.

For more information about breastfeeding, introducing solids and weaning, phone La Leche League (Great Britain) 0171 242 1278 or write to La Leche League (GB), BM 3424, London WC1N 3XX, to be put in touch with your nearest LLL Leader. With 150 Leaders in Great Britain, there is almost certainly someone near you, who can help.